THE POWERS OF THE PRESIDENCY

FINAL REPORT

ANNUAL CHIEF JUSTICE EARL WARREN

CONFERENCE ON ADVOCACY IN THE U.S.A.

JUNE 20 – JUNE 21, 1975

SORED BY THE ROSCOE POUND-AMERICAN TRIAL LAWYERS FOUNDATION

THE POWERS OF THE PRESIDENCY

FINAL REPORT

ANNUAL CHIEF JUSTICE EARL WARREN CONFERENCE
ON ADVOCACY IN THE UNITED STATES OF AMERICA

JUNE 20-21, 1975

Sponsored by

THE ROSCOE POUND-AMERICAN TRIAL LAWYERS FOUNDATION
20 Garden Street, Cambridge, Massachusetts 02138

Library of Congress Catalog Card Number: 75-32085

CONTENTS

Foreword

It is not beyond the intellect or resources of the American people once more to find and follow the polestar that led our forebearers to the creation of our Republic. These men of the 18th century were individuals who drew from their political experiences to form a government with *dispersed* power. This led to the first political experience of its kind: a government whose head was to be elected by its people.

The president of this newly-formed nation would not have unbridled power nor be arbitrary and absolute in performing his duties. However, as we celebrate the second centennial of the independence of this country, we are in the throes of recovering from one of the most crucial and extraordinary periods of this nation's political history.

What went awry that brought about a presidency to be referred to in phrases such as: "imperial presidency," "runaway presidency," "iniquitous presidency," "isolated presidency," "expanding presidency," "institutionalized presidency," among others?

Friday, August 9, 1974 saw the termination of the Nixon presidency. In aeons to come, our successors may note this as the date Americans realized the presidency had become the juggernaut that crippled the proper functioning of their government.

What legal guilt, moral nonresponsibility, malevolence there was in the Nixon Administration have been brought to the attention of the American public by those who have the responsibility to do so. And so it should be.

But, more importantly, there are men and women who are concerned with the role of the Executive as we move into the last quarter of the 20th century. It was to these highly knowledgeable people that this year's Annual Chief Justice Earl Warren

Conference on Advocacy was turned. The Conference topic was: The Powers of the Presidency. There were three areas of concentration – Presidential War Powers; Presidential Powers in Foreign Affairs; and Presidential Powers in Domestic Affairs.

The Conference was held, as in the past, at the Roscoe Pound-American Trial Lawyers Research Center in Cambridge, Massachusetts. The Conference called together 46 learned people from various scholarly pursuits but with complementary professional backgrounds. They assembled for two days on June 20 and June 21, 1975.

Three distinguished academicians, who have devoted their intellectual endeavors to passionately studying our system of government, prepared papers that served as background working papers for the Conference. We are indebted to them for their contribution.

They are: Professor Raoul Berger, Charles Warren Senior Fellow in American Legal History, Harvard Law School, who wrote on Presidential War Powers; Professor Louis Henkin, Hamilton Fish Professor of International Law and Diplomacy and Professor of Constitutional Law, Columbia University School of Law, who prepared the paper on Presidential Power in Foreign Affairs; and Professor Philip B. Kurland, William R. Kenan, Jr. Professor in the College and Professor of Law, University of Chicago Law School, whose paper is entitled "Toward a Responsible American Presidency" and directs his attention to presidential powers in domestic affairs.

In essence, their papers summarized their observations and recommendations for consideration by the Conference. These papers served as starting points for discussion. They are published herein, in their entirety, as significant works in themselves for future studies.

This invitational Conference brought together people who are presently working in government, or have served our government in a capacity that would give them insight into the workings of the Executive Branch of the government. Among the Conferees were journalists, political scientists, historians, law professors, Congressional assistants and a U.S. Representative. A number of these participants served in high-level sensitive government positions.

In order to foster intimate on-going discussions, the Conferees were assigned to one of three groups. The three areas of the topic were discussed separately with the writer of each background paper. Recommendations were formulated by each group and presented at a plenary session, at which time Final Recommendations were concluded.

We recognize that it is not an easy task to guide the direction of discussions toward reaching some conclusions within the limited time allowed by the Conference format. For being able to accomplish this so admirably, we extend our appreciation to those who served as group moderators: Professor Henry F. Graff, Professor of History, Columbia University; Professor Harvey C. Mansfield, Sr., Professor Emeritus of Government, Columbia University; Professor Adam Yarmolinsky, Ralph Waldo Emerson Professor of the University, University of Massachusetts.

An important phase of the Conference is to compile the Final Recommendations and the overall view of the Conferees. This most important function – a most difficult assignment – was accomplished very well by: Lawrence M. Baskir, General Counsel and Staff Director, President Ford's Clemency Board; Professor Harold W. Chase, Professor, Dept. of Political Science, University of Minnesota; and W. Taylor Reveley, III, Associate in the law firm, Hunton, Williams, Gay & Gibson in Richmond, Virginia and former International Affairs Fellow of the Council on Foreign Relations.

Following the two-day Conference, drafts of the Recommendations formulated were circulated by mail to all Conferees for their examination. This Report notes most of the additional explanations in footnotes.

> **It is important to keep in mind that this Conference sought a consensus. The Recommendations that follow represent a consensus of the Conference. They are not to be construed as the exact views of any particular Conferee.**

We have tried to convey the degree of acceptance by the Conferees of each Recommendation by stating the voting results during the plenary session.

This was a most stimulating and crucial Conference. In our Center people gathered who have warned of the veil of mysticism that has shrouded the highest office in the land.

These scholars know very well that the Executive Branch of our government, and other branches as well, must no longer delude themselves that our country has a favored destiny. Constant vigilance and revitalization of its governing institutions, in a constantly changing society, are of immediate concern. Winds of disturbance, whether economic or military, evidenced anywhere in the world, affect this nation. Because domestic affairs have become interwoven with foreign affairs, there is a compelling need for demystifying foreign diplomacy or foreign affairs for the public.

The Foundation does not advocate any particular stand taken in this Report. It serves as a convener to bring together people who give so generously of their learning in the awesome labor of seeking some answers. The Foundation is pleased to be able to publish the conclusions of the Conference. This Report will be distributed throughout the country to educational institutions, governmental agencies, news media, and various organizations. It is our intent to have it serve as a preface to further discussion and, whenever possible, to have its Recommendations and Findings seriously considered by those who have the responsibility to bring about change.

The Conference itself, and the publication of its conclusions, would not have been possible without the full support of our colleagues on the Board of the Roscoe Pound-American Trial Lawyers Foundation whom we have listed herein. To them we wish to extend our appreciation. Also we wish to acknowledge and extend our gratitude to our Foundation staff — Catherine E. Bentis, Executive Director, and Tobey Conlin, Assistant — who contributed so much toward the formulation of the Conference and the culmination of this publication.

To the Conferees who met with us in Cambridge, we wish to thank them for fully sharing their knowledge and personal vision on this crucial topic. We admire and respect each of them for engaging most earnestly in the hard work of finding new avenues for the functioning of the Presidency, drawn from their knowledge of history and from their firsthand experience.

We should listen to these voices of wisdom as we look forward to our third centenary of independence.

> Herbert H. Bennett
> *President,* The Roscoe Pound-American
> Trial Lawyers Foundation
> August 1972 - July 1975
>
> Theodore I. Koskoff
> *Chairman,* Annual Chief Justice
> Earl Warren Conference/1975
> President, The Roscoe Pound-American
> Trial Lawyers Foundation
> August 1975 -

FINAL REPORT

THE POWERS OF THE PRESIDENCY

PART A

RECOMMENDATIONS
PRESIDENTIAL WAR POWERS

Summary

(Note: Recommendations along with commentaries follow this summary. The War Powers Resolution is printed on pages 58-62 for your reference.)

The Conferees approached presidential war powers from a variety of perspectives. Attention was given to the extent of the Executive's actual control over American use-of-force decisions, as well as to what his control should be under the Constitution, the War Powers Resolution, and sound public policy. The Conferees differed in their factual, legal and policy conclusions — disagreeing more as to the reasons *why* the President's war powers ought to be of a certain nature, than as to *what* that nature, however, ought to be. What some felt to be constitutionally mandatory, for instance, others believed to be simply desirable as a matter of policy. Thus, the war powers Recommendations were framed to gather maximum support from those who agreed on result, even if they were at odds over rationale.

The Conferees defined the President's war powers in good part by reference to those of Congress. Emphasis on this measure of executive authority reflected consensus that Congress is still too little involved in American war-peace decisions. The Conference recognized that American use-of-force decisions are left almost wholly to presidential discretion when Congress remains silent. As the following Recommendations make clear, most Conferees favored a striking increase in congressional use-of-force influence and a corresponding decrease in presidential war powers, so as to encourage cooperation between the branches and to ensure checks and balances in the setting of American war-peace policy.

RECOMMENDATION I

Congress should participate more fully with the President in shaping American use-of-force policy than is now the case.

(Adopted overwhelmingly)

Commentary: The Conferees varied in their reasons why Congress should have greater influence that it now exerts over America's war-peace decisions. Some argued, for instance, that congressional control is constitutionally necessary. Others saw a link between congressional participation and national consensus, or a link between well-advised policy and the collective judgment of the President and Congress. Whatever their reasons, however, the Conferees agreed that the Executive continues to exercise disproportionate control over American use-of-force decisions — despite congressional termination of the country's Indochina involvement and despite congressional passage of the War Powers Resolution in 1973.[1]

---

1. Professor Louis Henkin wished the following noted, "I should say that I am not in sympathy with a number of recommendations or statements in the war powers section as I am not with *some* aspects of the War Powers Resolution, both on constitutional and political grounds."

RECOMMENDATION II

There must be systematic, continuing consultation between the President and Congress concerning use-of-force policy, as required by Section 3 of the War Powers Resolution.

(Adopted overwhelmingly)

(Note: Section 3 provides that: "The President in every possible instance shall consult with Congress before introducing United States Armed Forces into hostilities or into situations where imminent involvement in hostilities is clearly indicated by the circumstances, and after every such introduction shall consult regularly with the Congress until United States Armed Forces are no longer engaged in hostilities or have been removed from such situations.")

Commentary: The Conferees agreed that consulation should be a meaty process as described by the U.S. House Committee on International Relations in these terms: "Rejected was the notion that consultation should be synonymous with merely being informed. Rather, consultation . . . means that a decision is pending on a problem and that Members of Congress are being asked by the President for their advice and opinions and, in appropriate circumstances, their approval of action contemplated. Furthermore, for consultation to be meaningful, the President himself must participate and all information relevant to the situation must be made available." (H.R. Rep. No. 287, 93d Cong., 1st Sess. [1973], 2 U.S. Code & Ad. News 2351 [1973].)

RECOMMENDATION III

Congress should provide greater legislative direction to the deployment of American armed forces abroad when their imminent involvement in hostilities is NOT clearly indicated by the circumstances.

(Adopted by substantial majority)

Commentary: The War Powers Resolution requires that the President report to Congress any deployment of American armed forces: "into the territory, airspace or waters of a foreign nation, while equipped for combat, except for deployments which relate solely to supply, replacement, repair, or training of such forces; or in numbers which substantially enlarge United States Armed Forces equipped for combat already located in a foreign nation."

Against this background, the Conferees urge Congress to pay more attention to the circumstances in which American armed forces are placed abroad, including as appropriate the passage of legislation authorizing, limiting or ending particular deployments. The Conference recognized that deployments which do not initially risk imminent involvement in hostilities can nonetheless lead to later involvement.

RECOMMENDATION IV

The President should neither deploy American armed forces into situations where imminent involvement in hostilities is clearly indicated by the circumstances, nor should he commit them to actual hostilities, except pursuant to (1) a declaration of war, (2) other specific statutory authorization, or (3) a national emergency created by attack upon the United States, its territories or possessions, or its armed forces.[1]

(Adopted by narrow margin)

Commentary: Some Conferees who supported this Recommendation would have preferred that the phrase "or its armed forces" be omitted, on the ground that the phrase suggests undue capacity for unilateral Executive action. Most Conferees who opposed the Recommendation, on the other hand, objected to its limited view of when the President should be free to take military steps without prior congressional approval.

The text of this Recommendation essentially sets forth the language of Section 2 (c) of the War Powers Resolution. Congress, however, has not given Section 2 (c) any operative effect. The Section simply states congressional belief about the nature of the President's constitutional war powers.[2]

---

1. Professor Adam Yarmolinsky believes "the inclusion of the phrase 'or its armed forces' largely vitiates the restraints proposed here and I would omit that phrase, *assuming* that 'other specific statutory authorization' includes ratified treaties where U.S. military response is contemplated – *e.g.* NATO."

2. Professor Gerhard Casper disagrees strongly with the above commentary. He states, "The Resolution says nowhere that Section 2 (c) shall not have operational effect. Sections 4ff all make perfect sense if the 2 (c) restrictions are read into them. Section 2 is clearly part of a legally binding resolution." He further commented, "Even if the proper reading of the Resolution were as suggested, I do not believe the President has constitutional power to introduce forces unless authorized in the way envisaged by Section 2 (c). In short, I find that Section to put forward what is the proper constitutional principle."

Professor Philip B. Kurland concurs with Professor Casper's view.

RECOMMENDATION V

Congress should amend the War Powers Resolution to give Section 2 (c) operative effect.[1]

(Adopted by narrow margin)

(*Note:* Section 2 (c) states: "The constitutional powers of the President as Commander-in-Chief to introduce United States Armed Forces into hostilities, or into situations where imminent involvement in hostilities is clearly indicated by the circumstances, are exercised only pursuant to (1) a declaration of war, (2) specific statutory authorization, or (3) a national emergency created by attack upon the United States, its territories or possessions, or its armed forces.")

Commentary: Although Section 2 (c) expressly defines Executive authority, the Conference believed that Congress disregarded the Section by adopting other provisions of the War Powers Resolution which permit the President to enter hostilities as he thinks best, so long as he promptly reports to the legislators, obtains their approval within sixty days, and meets certain other conditions. This Recommendation would have Congress implement Section 2 (c).[2]

---

1. Professor Casper disagrees sharply with this Recommendation for the reasons stated on the previous page.
2. Professor Harvey C. Mansfield, Sr. interprets Section 2 (c) "as an expression of congressional opinion — overwhelming opinion, to be sure, at the time — thrust upon the President by overriding his veto; but an opinion nevertheless which he can disregard, albeit at his peril."

RECOMMENDATION VI

The President should be free to protect American citizens attacked abroad when the rescue effort is proportionate to the attack and involves little risk of the country's involvement in significant hostilities, provided that there take place all the Congressional-Executive consultation that the circumstances permit.

(Adopted by narrow margin)

Commentary: This Recommendation would give the President more military freedom than suggested by Recommendations IV and V. However, only under limited circumstances. The Conferees rejected by a substantial majority a proposal that the President be permitted on his own authority to introduce American armed forces into hostilities so long as he reports to Congress within 48 hours after their introduction and submits to any limitation or termination of his action that may be voted by congressional concurrent resolution.

Mayaguez Incident

As some Conferees believed that the full Mayaguez facts have yet to emerge, they were reluctant to judge Executive use of force during the incident. Other Conferees concluded that the President's military action had both rescue and reprisal aspects, each with different implications for the proper scope of Executive action. The Conferees were divided in a vote on whether the President's use of American armed forces during the Mayaguez incident exceeded his appropriate war powers.[1]

---

1. Mr. Theodore I. Koskoff wished it noted that, in the Mayaguez incident, the President distinctly claims his power to use armed forces was not under the War Powers Resolution but on his so-called constitutional power. Mr. Koskoff further comments, "It is my view that the President had no such constitutional power to act as he did in this incident."

RECOMMENDATION VII

Whatever the limits on the President's OVERT commitment of American armed forces to hostilities, the same limits should govern his COVERT commitment of armed forces to hostilities, whether these forces are American or foreign, and whether or not they are part of the regular military.

(Adopted overwhelmingly)

RECOMMENDATION VIII

Congress should develop the capacity for periodic review of American use-of-force policy and for participation with the President in its shaping even during crisis situations. For example, the legislators should:

A) Conduct a comprehensive, annual analysis of the country's war-peace circumstances, with particular emphasis on treaty and troop commitments;

B) Create a Joint Congressional Consultation Committee to advise the President during military emergencies until such time as Congress as a whole has had an opportunity to act.[1]

(Adopted overwhelmingly)

---

1. Mr. Sanford J. Ungar would stipulate that the membership of any congressional group, such as the Congressional Committee suggested above, "should be a rotating one, and the length of time that any one member of Congress can serve on it restricted (say to eight years). Otherwise, I think it would be virtually impossible to avoid the cooptation and rubber-stamping that have characterized past congressional efforts at oversight and consultation in these areas."

Commentary: The Conferees recognized that the Joint Congressional Consultation Committee recommended here, and the Executive-Congressional Policy Group suggested in Recommendation XI in the Section, PRESIDENTIAL POWERS IN FOREIGN AFFAIRS, in this Report, would serve closely-related functions, and thus should be merged. The members of each must be well-schooled in military and diplomatic affairs if they are to consult meaningfully with the highly-informed Executive. The best preparation for informed membership on the emergency Joint Congressional Consultation Committee, in fact, would be service on the Policy Group. It was thought that this Group should remain small in order to have productive exchange with the Executive.

RECOMMENDATION IX

Each individual member of Congress should resolve to stay sufficiently informed about pertinent developments to vote intelligently — yea or nay on war-peace issues.

(Adopted overwhelmingly)

Commentary: The Conferees felt it very important that each member of Congress take personal responsibility for informed participation with the President in shaping American use-of-force policy. The willingness of individual senators and representatives to assume that responsibility, in the Conferees' opinion, is essential to congressional influence over American war-peace policy.[1]

---

1. Professor Anthony A. D'Amato expressed the opinion that Recommendations I, II, VIII and IX would be ineffectual unless a Congressional resolution were adopted, which stated that "(a) any Joint Congressional Consultation Committee must meet as a whole with the President and any sub-group of such Committee should refuse to meet with the President unless the invitation is open to the entire membership of the Committee; and/or (b) Congress shall not be deemed to have been informed of any foreign-policy matter initiated or conducted by the Executive if the President informs only a person or sub-group selected by him of the relevant Committee that was entitled to such information."

PART B

RECOMMENDATIONS
PRESIDENTIAL POWERS IN FOREIGN AFFAIRS

Summary

The Conference discussions established that in the participants' view there was much in the exercise of Presidential power in foreign affairs to cause legitimate concern. It was the consensus that too often the most important and crucial decisions in foreign policy-making were made unilaterally by the Executive Branch — from the agreements at Yalta to the "tilting" of recent administrations. It was felt that it would be more faithful to the Spirit of the Constitution to include a systematic, substantial, and efficacious Congressional "in-put" into foreign policy-making. There were no illusions that this would be an easy task to accomplish — human nature and the political process of democracy being what they are. The Conference concluded that the best that could be sought was change which would give greater promise of sane and wise foreign policy decisions for the future by broader participation in policy-making.

One overriding concern of the Conference was the need for a complete national examination of the goals and guidelines in foreign affairs in the hope of reaching a national consensus, taking into account the new significance of economic factors, particularly food, fuel and finance.

Specific recommendations to meet concerns about foreign policy-making revolved around improving the operations of both the Executive Branch and the Legislative Branch, as well as Executive-Legislative relationships. The principal changes recommended are in Congressional-Executive relationships and in the changes within Congress to make them effective. These changes address themselves primarily to three major functions:

  a. Congressional participation in policy-making.
  b. Congressional oversight.
  c. Congressional access to information.

RECOMMENDATION X

A special Executive-Legislative Group should be formed immediately to examine the goals of U.S. foreign policy and the guidelines for the conduct of foreign affairs in order to re-establish a national consensus.[1]

(Adopted overwhelmingly)

Commentary: It was felt that in the past there had been a national consensus relative to foreign policy, which had been reflected in presidential actions. In recent years, however, the President has followed a course in the absence of national consensus and, furthermore, he has not been sufficiently concerned with seeking such a consensus.

It was the Conference's belief that there is an urgent need for a complete examination of foreign policy goals and guidelines for the conduct of foreign affairs. The Conferees stressed that special emphasis of such an examination should be placed on economic factors, in particular those relating to food, fuel and finance.[2]

---

1. Dr. Thomas E. Cronin did not think that such a new group is needed. Congressional foreign affairs committees should handle this work. Dr. Cronin felt, too, that the above outlined proposal would in practice resemble those all too familiar ineffective presidential advisory commissions.

Professor Arthur M. Schlesinger, Jr. fears that a special Executive-Legislative Group would be unproductive.

2. Professor Adam Yarmolinsky, who served as one of the Conference Moderators, observed that the Conferees were aware of the weakening distinction between the powers of the President in domestic affairs and foreign affairs. He concludes, "Foreign policy is more and more an aspect of almost every domestic policy problem, rather than a distinct field of concern. Decisions about domestic, industrial and agricultural production, monetary and fiscal policy, control of scarce resources and protection of the environment, all impinge to a greater or lesser degree on the rest of the world, as decisions on these matters taken outside the United States impinge on our domestic affairs. These interrelationships make it more difficult to generalize separately about the presidential powers in either area, and more importantly to see presidential power in the total context of government activity."

RECOMMENDATION XI

A permanent Executive-Congressional Policy Group should be established to meet regularly for private discussions, in addition to existing forms of Congressional participation in foreign affairs policy-making.

(Adopted overwhelmingly)

Commentary: The Conference recognized that abuses exist in the exercise of executive power. Suggestions for remedies centered on improving the operations of the Executive Branch, the Legislative Branch and the Executive-Legislative relationships.

A regular, institutionalized Executive-Congressional Policy Group was recommended as a principal vehicle for improved Congressional participation. Such a Group could be composed of the leaders of both political parties in the House and Senate, plus the chairmen and ranking minority members of the Senate and House Armed Services Committees, the Senate Foreign Relations Committee and the House International Relations Committee.[1] This Policy Group should hold weekly meetings with the President and selected officials in the Executive Branch. The purpose is to have a continuing and systematic relationship in which Congressional leaders would participate with the Executive Branch in the process of foreign policy formulation. Such a Group, of course, would not be a panacea; hope is that it would both improve decision-making and give Congress an opportunity to participate early and affirmatively rather than only as an adversary, after the fact.

---

1. Professor Schlesinger pointed out, "This might be worth trying, but the designated congressional members of the group are precisely the corps of tired elder statesmen most inclined to defer to the executive in the field of foreign policy."

RECOMMENDATION XII

For intelligence and related operations, a Joint Congressional Committee should be established modeled on the Joint Committee on Atomic Energy, with rotating personnel, charged with both continuing scrutiny as well as holding an annual review of intelligence activities.

(Adopted overwhelmingly)

Commentary: The Conference felt strongly that recent disclosures involving the activities of the C.I.A. and other intelligence agencies demonstrate dramatically the need for genuine Congressional oversight of such agencies. To avoid co-optation of Congressional committees by the agencies they are charged with overseeing, it was regarded as important to have rotation of membership on the Committee. [Note: The Joint Committee on Atomic Energy was created in 1946 to oversee the activities of the Atomic Energy Commission. The legislation establishing the Joint Committee required that "The Commission shall keep the joint committee *fully* and currently informed with respect to all of the Commission's activities." (Emphasis added.)]

It is generally acknowledged that the Joint Committee has performed well in maintaining oversight and in exercising discretion with respect to sensitive and secret information with which it has been supplied by the Commission.[1] It was felt that this specific Joint Committee could serve as a model for this Recommendation.

---

1. Professor Anthony A. D'Amato dissents from this statement. He feels that a Joint Congressional Committee, modeled on the Joint Committee on Atomic Energy, would "become the tool of the agency it is supposed to watch."

RECOMMENDATION XIII

A small corps of congressional liaison officers should be established to serve with the State Department, the Department of Defense and other selected agencies involved in the conduct of foreign affairs.[1]

(Adopted by narrow margin)

Commentary: The majority of Conferees agreed that, in addition to the existing forms, it would be helpful to have a corps of liaison officers operating within Executive agencies. This would enhance congressional information-gathering and understanding about foreign policy and process. Such a corps would give Congress better access to developments in those agencies than is currently available to it. Also, it was felt that the efficacy of such a liaison corps is attested to by the effectiveness with which Executive agencies use liaison officers to keep abreast of developments in Congress.

---

1. Dr. Cronin thinks it unnecessary and undesirable to establish a small corps of congressional liaison officers. He states: "Congress should instead use its quite ample hearings, oversight and investigative powers to achieve the same objective."

Professor Harvey C. Mansfield, Sr. disagrees, stating: "The Foreign Relations and International Relations committees already have staffs for this purpose, among others. Every member has a staff allowance and can use some of it in this field if he/she feels the need. The leadership in both houses does not have subject matter specialist staffs. Unless this tradition is reversed it is not at all clear who the 'liaison officers' would be working for. If it were reversed, this would mark a major power shift within the houses of Congress."

Mr. Jerrold L. Schecter comments: "A corps of congressional liaison officers would clog the bureaucratic channels that now exist, run across the the lines of the existing congressional committees which work with the State and Defense departments and add a layer of unfocused and undirected personnel to the already existing framework for consultation between the legislative and executive. This recommendation lacks the functional utility that the permanent Executive-Congressional Policy Group, as suggested in Recommendation XI, would have as well as the expanded staff for the foreign relations and international relations committees. The problem, in my experience, has been that the Senate and House committees dealing with foreign policy have not fully utilized the information generated by staffers, especially the excellent staff of the Senate Foreign Relations Committee. The problem is not more people and generating information but the attention span and follow through of Congressmen."

RECOMMENDATION XIV

Congress should acquire sufficient staff proficient in foreign affairs so that it would have its own expertise on important substantive matters including knowledge and understanding of foreign geographical areas and issues.[1]

(Adopted overwhelmingly)

Commentary: It was the judgment of the Conference that Congress needs foreign policy analysts of its own to enhance the sources of information for Congress on substantive foreign policy issues. This would be at least something on the order of the Congressional Budget Office.

[Note: In 1974, in order "to improve congressional control of budget outlays," the Congress established budget committees in both the House and Senate, as well as a Congressional Budget Office.]

Although it is too soon to make judgments about the efficacy of these committees and the Office in the budgeting process, most Conferees felt that there was merit in the approach and that it should be applied in foreign affairs, where the need for Congressional expertise is also of crucial importance.

A significant number of Conferees wanted to specify that the added staff should be assigned to the International Relations and Foreign Relations Committees. However, others felt that where the staff was to be assigned should be left to the discretion of Congress.

---

1. Professor Mansfield disagrees with this Recommendation and states: "Congress is already congested with staff. A congressional staff in foreign affairs can't match the executive without access to daily cables and other classified material. These may be shown to members and a selected few staff of relevant committees, but not to any numerous general-purpose staff agency like the Congressional Budget Office."

RECOMMENDATION XV

Generally full information should be given to Congress, if necessary on a classified basis, for the needs of confidentiality of the Executive Branch and of the diplomatic process do not ordinarily require withholding information from Congress.[1]

(Adopted overwhelmingly)

Commentary: A Recommendation proposing the absolute prohibition of the executive privilege was rejected. The discussion indicated widespread opinions — from the view that there was no such thing as a legitimate executive privilege to the position that national security and interest *required* such a privilege, prudently exercised.[2] The consensus, however, was that *generally* Congress should be given all the information it needs to perform its legislating, appropriating and overseeing functions effectively but that there would be occasions where information should and could be legitimately withheld or given subject only to special safeguards.[3]

---

1. Professor Yarmolinsky states: "I would distinguish sharply between a) executive privilege, i.e. the privilege of decision-makers in the executive branch (and legislators too, for that matter) to receive confidential advice from anyone they wish to consult, and to insist that the confidentiality of that be protected, so that its honesty is not compromised; and b) withholding of information on security grounds, where I believe the executive must surrender to the legislative branch any information sought, under appropriate safeguards, and must make provisions to inform appropriate individuals within the legislative branch (leadership of both parties, relevant committee chairmen) of classified activities."

2. Mr. Theodore I. Koskoff dissents with the view that there is any such valid constitutional doctrine as "Executive Privilege" as it is applied to the Congress. He states: "The notion advanced by the adherents to the doctrine that it exists by implication; otherwise the President would be obliged to commute from the White House to the Congress presupposes an irresponsible Congress. History does not support this view and the fact is that Presidents have often been irresponsible and the Congress seldom, if ever, irresponsible."

3. Mr. Malcolm D. Hawk would further add to this commentary: "Congress has an equal responsibility to treat this information in appropriate fashion in order to demonstrate its ability to handle classified material. If necessary discipline of members should be sanctioned if rules of confidentiality are not observed."

Ms. Irene R. Margolis rejects the notion that *"generally* Congress should

RECOMMENDATION XVI

Congress should organize itself so that it uses effectively the information it receives.[1]

(Adopted overwhelmingly)

Commentary: It was pointed out that Congress already receives a great volume of information with respect to the conduct of foreign policy but that often it does not use the information or use it effectively. For example, under the Case Act, Congress currently receives copies of Executive Agreements — but apparently there is no standardized procedure for systematically reviewing those Agreements, and considering possible action.[2]

---

be given all information it needs to perform its legislating, appropriating and overseeing functions." She further explains: "There can be no such qualification if Congress is to be expected to function effectively. I can perceive of *no* instance where any government information should be withheld from Congress. If a President is permitted absolute discretion as to what information he provides Congress and under what circumstances, then Congressional oversight is rendered meaningless and dominance of the Executive Branch is assured.

"An unfettered flow of information to Congress is fundamental to our system of checks and balances. Any proposal which would encourage the suppression of information by the Executive Branch should be vigorously resisted."

1. Professor Mansfield explained: "It is hopeless to ask that everyone be informed about everything. Proper organization, then, suggests that a few committee members master a given specialty and tell the other members how to vote on their bills. The only information the other members would then need is the identity of their specialist and the cue he gives."

2. See the comments on this Recommendation by Ms. Margolis which follow this section of the Report. (Page 28.)

RECOMMENDATION XVII

**A small agency on the General Accounting Office model should be
established to scrutinize the Executive bureaucracy in foreign
affairs.**[1]

(Adopted overwhelmingly)

Commentary: With regard to oversight, it was felt that a small agency on the General
Accounting Office model would be helpful in spot-checking all of the agencies
involved in foreign affairs activity, including the Departments of State and Defense,
the United States Information Agency, the Central Intelligence Agency (C.I.A.) and
the like.

[Note: The General Accounting Office, created in 1921, has *audit* authority
over virtually all departments and agencies of the Federal government for the
purpose of "providing legislative control over the receipt, disbursement, and
application of public funds."]

It was felt that it would be advantageous to have, in addition to the General
Accounting Office, an agency which "audited" the *substance* of the activities of
agencies involved in foreign affairs.

This agency should be free to examine at will any specific activity of the
agencies involved in foreign affairs. One Conferee was of the opinion that this
agency should be given the authority to do an on-the-spot "audit" — without prior
notice — of a Department's or agency's activities.

---

1. Dr. Cronin disagrees. He feels strongly that foreign affairs and government
operations committees should be charged with these responsibilities. He feels too
that this and similar proposals will merely create a bureaucratized legislative branch
overly burdened with organizational problems of its own. He fears that too many
added layers of advisory units on Capitol Hill will weaken rather than strengthen the
oversight and representative functions of the Congress.

Professor Mansfield disagrees with this Recommendation, stating: "Such an
agency would be in continuous jurisdictional rivalry with GAO and Foreign
Relations committee staff, would not get access to classified material and would
only add to the congestion of staff."

RECOMMENDATION XVIII

An Executive Council should be established comprised of four or five distinguished citizens who will serve as full-time advisors to the President.[1]

(Adopted by narrow margin)

Commentary: The Conferees thought it important to improve policy-making within the Executive Branch. An Executive Council was suggested in order to provide high-level advice from outside the Executive Branch. It was considered important that knowledgeable people of prestige and distinction should be appointed by the President with the advice and consent of the Senate.[2]

---

1. Professor Mansfield believes that, as desirable as it may be for the President to have an Executive Council, which would be a group of advisers, "there is no way to make him use it if he doesn't want to, or finds them uncongenial. Confirmation by the Senate implies a statue." Professor Mansfield further believes that this "recommendation needs rather to be addressed to the President; if he is persuaded, he needn't wait for a statute" to establish an Executive Council. He felt the President could get the same result by appointing advisers who would serve as Ambassadors-at-large and sending their names to the Senate. He concludes: "These would be in effect cabinet members without departments."

Professor Yarmolinsky would not "formalize the advice-seeking or advice-giving process within the executive. Decision-makers, up to and including the President, should be free to decide what advice they want and how they want it."

2. Professor J. David Greenstone fully agrees with the Recommendation and commentary and would further add that "by bringing such persons of independent stature to the White House we may slightly decrease the 'Imperial' nature of the Presidency."

RECOMMENDATION XIX

**The President should involve Congress in advance in the deliberations
and decision-making process before he enters into long-term
commitments to foreign governments entailing substantial costs.**

(Adopted overwhelmingly)

Commentary: The Conference recognized that the President has some constitutional
authority to enter into international obligations that commit public funds. The
President's authority to recognize a foreign government, for example, entails certain
costs. But Presidents claim authority to make other, farther-reaching commitments
involving substantial financial military and other costs. For that reason, there was
concern that a President should involve Congress in advance, particularly since the
Conference felt that it was both unseemly and irresponsible for Congress to fail to
honor the commitments of the President. At the same time, it was felt that there
should be some way of holding the President accountable.

Comments on Recommendation XVI
Ms. Irene R. Margolis

Admittedly Congress is at a disadvantage when dealing with foreign policy
information. But the disadvantage is one created and perpetrated by Executive
Branch policies. One must bear in mind the restrictions under which the Congress is
forced to operate.

The Executive Branch controls the flow of foreign policy information to
Congress. While the Foreign Relations Committee routinely receives a great deal of
information from the Executive Branch, the vast majority of that information is of
marginal importance. Presidents have deliberately withheld, censored or manipulated
information crucial to Congressional deliberations on foreign policy. Consider the
Ford Administration's conduct with regard to the latest Middle East withdrawal
agreement. Four separate "Memoranda of Agreement" were concluded — three with
the Government of Israel and one with the Egyptian Government. Despite the
nature and extent of the assurances contained in these arguments, only one narrow
provision was submitted to the Congress for specific approval. That was, of course,

the proposal for stationing U.S. technicians in the Sinai to monitor the Early Warning System.

Yet the State Department's Legal Adviser, Monroe Leigh, maintained a formal opinion filed in a letter dated September 18, 1975, to the House International Relations Committee, that the two binding agreements would go into force after Congress had acted on the proposal to place technicians in the Sinai. He asserted that these two Memoranda of Agreement were "properly described under United States constitutional practice as executive agreements" and that it was "clear" that when executed, the agreements "will become international agreements." He rejected the need for Congressional approval of the supplementary Memoranda of Agreements because while the undertakings were binding, in his opinion, they " . . .fall in the category either of those which the President is already authorized to make under existing legislation or under the traditional powers of the President to make statements of political intention in the conduct of foreign affairs."

Without debating here the specific Sinai proposal or my position with regard to the use of executive agreements in the instant case, I would submit that this controversy underscores the fundamental problem facing Congress when it attempts to assert itself in the foreign policy area.

The Case Act was a first step in trying to get some control over the use and scope of executive agreements so that the Congress would be fully and currently informed of our foreign commitments. As such it was a modest first step. All the Case Act requires is that the executive submit the text of all executive agreements within 60 days after they are concluded. The Case Act does not provide for approval or disapproval action by the Congress. (That is the aim of the Bentsen and Glenn bills, S. 632 and S. 1251 respectively, which are currently pending before the Senate Subcommittee on Separation of Powers.) Consistent with the provisions of the Case Act, the following review procedure has been established by the Foreign Relations Committee: Upon receipt of the text of a newly concluded executive agreement, the Committee staff prepares an analysis of the agreement and includes a summary of the agreement in the committee's Weekly Report to its members. The Agreement and supporting documentation are kept on file for review by the members.

Inasmuch as no positive Congressional action is contemplated within the terms of the Case Act, I am not quite sure what lack of action this Recommendation is directed toward. Perhaps the lack of public knowledge about committee action on executive agreements is more a manifestation of the subject matter of what is submitted as an executive agreement rather than a lack of review by the committee. There is the belief in many quarters that the Executive Branch is avoiding the law requiring the reporting of all executive agreements, by concluding the more controversial commitments in other forms, such as agency-to-agency contracts. Until the Executive Branch provides Congress with *all* pertinent information, irrespective of the label that it places on the information, Congress will never be able to deal effectively with foreign policy information.

PART C

RECOMMENDATIONS
PRESIDENTIAL POWERS IN DOMESTIC AFFAIRS

Summary

It was the consensus of the Conference that the American presidency has accumulated too much power in domestic affairs.[1] It was concluded that, in our constitutional system of government, this concentration of power in the Executive Branch of the government was undesirable and contrary to the spirit and history of our republic.

Although the Conferees recognized the need for a powerful presidency in the modern era, they felt that the pendulum had swung too far toward a strong presidency, thus upsetting the checks and balances of our form of government.[2]

The Conference was unanimous in the view that no constitutional changes were necessary or desirable as a response to the problem of excessive executive power. It turned most of its attention to Congress. The Conference agreed that a primary avenue for controlling inordinate power in domestic affairs was in improving Congress' ability to perform its oversight responsibilities.

---

1. Professor Arthur M. Schlesinger, Jr. expressed the opinion: "In my view the President has too much power in some areas in domestic policy, too little in others (e.g., the President should have the power within designated limits to vary tax rates in response to changing economic conditions)."

2. Professor Schlesinger believes, "The pendulum has swung too far because of the requirements, read or imagined, of international crisis; not for reasons of domestic policy."

The Conferees unanimously agreed that Congress should increase its ability to oversee more effectively the activities of the President and the Executive Branch.

By an overwhelming majority the Conferees agreed that abuses, such as those which surfaced during the investigation of the Watergate Affair, are more apt to occur with the existence of a large group of officials in the President's immediate entourage who are able to act in the name of the President, but who are not politically responsible nor responsive to Congress or the public. The Conference concluded that reforms are necessary to reduce and control the exercise of independent power by these officials in the White House and the Executive Office of the President.

While the Conference was in agreement on the potential dangers of having presidential assistants acting outside normal constraints, many Conferees believed this to be a problem peculiar to the Nixon Administration. Substantial sentiment was expressed on the need of the President to have assistants loyal to and identified with him. Otherwise, the President could not enforce his policies on the permanent machinery of the Executive Branch, which has its own institutional biases. Nonetheless, the Conference believed firmly that constant care is necessary to control the power, limit the number and increase the accountability of the President's assistants.

There was limited discussion on the method of filling a vacancy in the Office of the Vice President, as set forth in the Second Article of the 25th Amendment to the U.S. Constitution. A majority of the Conferees were critical of the present system of having the President nominate and Congress confirm a successor in the case of a vacancy in the Office of the Vice President, and of his possible succession to the Office of the President. A proposal was made that, in case of a vacancy in the Office of the Vice President, succession should be determined by a special election. This received strong support. However, the Conference was not prepared to elaborate on this proposal or to suggest other alternatives.

A proposal that the Office of the Vice President be abolished was overwhelmingly rejected.

Following are Recommendations that reflect the consensus of the Conferees in attempting to restore the balance between these two branches of government.

RECOMMENDATION XX

Congress should have a centralized office for the collection of information for oversight purposes. This body, which might be called the Office of Legal Counsel of Congress, would have the power to examine the operation of any government agency, including intelligence agencies.[1]

(Adopted overwhelmingly)

Commentary: The Conference agreed that the Congressional committee system does not provide sufficient continuity or expertise in the oversight function, in large part because the staffs are subject to the direction of senior members with particular interests and changing priorities. As a result, committees are excessively dependent on information gathered from the executive agencies under examination. Creating a central oversight office would provide committees with independent information and technical resources with which to pursue their oversight objectives, much as the General Accounting Office (GAO) functions.

---

1. Professor Harvey C. Mansfield, Sr. pointed out two difficulties with this Recommendation: "1) Jurisdictional boundaries between this office and GAO. 2) Who would this office be working for? Somebody must be authorized to tell it to move in here, and stay away there. GAO has an automatic grist of vouchers and accounts coming to it, with a statutory duty to examine them. Its statutory discretion to investigate anything on its own initiative rests on this body of operations. No comparable guides are given this proposed new office."

Professor David R. Mayhew believes that this office is unnecessary and unworkable.

Professor Schlesinger comments: "I am skeptical. Such an office would probably find itself in endless jurisdictional conflict with the standing committees."

Professor Adam Yarmolinsky states: "I am not convinced that a new entity is required to perform this function outside the GAO."

RECOMMENDATION XXI

The Office of Legal Counsel of the Congress should be empowered also to represent the legislative interest of Congress in civil litigation when the Justice Department does not.[1]

(Adopted overwhelmingly)

RECOMMENDATION XXII

Part of each congressional committee staff now in existence or established in the future should be composed of permanent professional employees who are not subject to the political patronage of the chairman or of any other individual committee member.[2]

(Adopted overwhelmingly)

Commentary: A small number of committee staffs are presently comprised of highly-qualified professionals who are hired by the full committee, not by individual members. However, changes in committee membership result in a reconstitution of the entire staff in most committees. The Conferees agreed that making a part of each committee staff permanent and responsible to the entire committee will provide desirable continuity, knowledge and experience, and will still make it possible for the new committee chairman and members to address new objectives.

---

1. Professor Mansfield disagrees. He states, "The occasions for congressional litigation are infrequent; no new permanent agency is needed. Existing arrangements are flexible and adequate to handle special occasions."
2. Professor Mansfield comments: "The Legislative Reorganization acts already direct this; the trouble is, too many members don't want it to apply to them, and there is no effective and ready means of enforcement."

RECOMMENDATION XXIII

A permanent Office of Special Prosecutor should NOT be created for the purpose of investigating or prosecuting wrong-doing by the Executive Branch staff.

(Adopted by narrow margin)

Commentary: **The Conference rejected the proposal to establish a permanent Special Prosecutor's Office,** such as the one that came into being during the Watergate investigation.[1] Some Conferees believed that there were adequate resources within the U.S. Justice Department capable and trustworthy to perform whatever investigatory or prosecutorial duties were required relative to any illegalities on the part of the Executive Branch, and that unusual situations would better be handled *ad hoc,* as in Watergate.[2]

---

1. Professor J. David Greenstone noted that a permanent office would no longer be "special." He added that "special" prosecutors should be appointed — as in Watergate — only under special circumstances.

2. Professor Yarmolinsky would add that "the investigative function of Congressional committees supplements the function of the Dept. of Justice."

Professor Anthony A. D'Amato comments, "initiative and vigilence in the Dept. of Justice might be sapped if there were an independent Office charged with such matters. However, it should be stressed that the Dept. of Justice represents the government as a whole and not simply the Executive."

RECOMMENDATION XXIV

No member of the Executive Branch, regardless of status, title or function, should have the right to appear before Congress when summoned to testify.

(Adopted overwhelmingly)

Commentary: The Conferees noted that this does not apply to the President nor, presumably, to the Vice President, in which cases the court-adjudicated limits of subpoena power would apply.[1]

---

1. Mr. Malcolm D. Hawk adds: "While being required to appear, members of the personal staffs of the President and Vice-President could not be required to testify against the instructions of the President."

Professor Schlesinger states: "I think the same immunity should extend to those members of the White House staff whose only duty is to advise the President — i.e., who have no significant operational functions. And it should apply to the content of advice given personally to the President, from whatever source."

RECOMMENDATION XXV

Congress should define by statute the scope and substance of any Executive right to withhold information from Congress.

(Adopted overwhelmingly)

Any statute defining the right to withhold information should be limited to the following areas:

A)   **Advice given to a superior;**

(Adopted overwhelmingly)

B)   **Military secrets;**

(Adopted overwhelmingly)

C)   **Matters relating to criminal investigations;**

(Adopted overwhelmingly)

D)   **Intelligence.**

(Adopted by narrow margin)

Commentary: It was the consensus of the Conference that any Executive right to withhold information should be a matter of legislative definition rather than Executive declaration. However, interestingly enough, there were strongly-held opinions as to whether or not there existed "Executive privilege" regarding the right to withhold information. Many participants took the position that no "Executive privilege" exists under the Constitution.

Although the Conference concluded that exceptions should be limited to the four specified areas, it was the common understanding that Congress should define the exact dimensions of each of the exceptions.[1]

---

1. Professor Yarmolinsky stated: "I believe that there should be provisions for matters under (B) and (D) to be shared with appropriate Congressional officials (leadership, some committee chairmen)."

Professor Mansfield makes the following observation: "This is a pious hope. No statutory definitions could be so clear and specific as to be self-executing. No President is likely to agree that Congress, except by impeachment, can unilaterally

Dissent from Recommendation XXV
Ms. Irene R. Margolis

Other than the narrow personal privilege accorded a President in order to protect confidential advice he receives from a personal adviser, the President does not now have, nor should he be given, the right to withhold any government information from Congress. I view with great alarm any statute which seeks to establish permissible categories of government information which can per se be withheld from Congress. Permissible exceptions from disclosure immediately become absolute categories of information to be withheld, and all information the least bit sensitive invariably falls within the excepted classes. Additionally, such a statutory exception would become authority for the Executive Branch to withhold all information in any given category. Experience with the Freedom of Information Act exceptions vividly demonstrates this to be so.

There is, in my opinion, no information pertaining to the functioning of government which can or should be withheld from Congress. "Classified" or sensitive information is precisely the information Congress must regularly receive if it is to execute faithfully its responsibilities under the Constitution and function as a co-equal branch of government. It is ludicrous to expect Congress to legislate effectively if the Executive branch withholds the most crucial government information from Congressional review.

What should be established is not a privilege to withhold information from Congress, but rather a process by which Congress is regularly and fully informed on all matters of government policy and decisions. As demonstrated by the record of the Joint Atomic Energy Committee, such a process is not unrealistic or unattainable, and the benefits are immediately apparent.

The difficult period we are experiencing in our country today is a direct result of the obsession for secrecy which permeated the Executive branch in previous administrations. For myriad reasons, which included national security, military secrets, intelligence, confidentiality and separation of powers, substantial information bearing on questionable governmental activities was withheld not only from the public but from Congressional scrutiny. I cannot support any proposal which would condone such unwarranted withholding of information from Congress.

---

determine the extent of the President's duty to disclose, e.g. President Ford and Congressman Otis Pike's committee just now." [Congressman Pike is chairman of the U.S. House Select Committee on Intelligence.]

RECOMMENDATION XXVI

Congress should define by statute the standards for classification and declassification of information that will serve as guidelines for principal agencies of the government.[1]

(Adopted overwhelmingly)

RECOMMENDATION XXVII

All directors of offices within the Executive Office of the President should be subject to Senate confirmation, with functions and budgets prescribed by law.

(Adopted overwhelmingly)

Commentary: The Conference was of the view that the directors of miscellaneous agencies grouped under the Executive Office of the President — such as the Office of Management and Budget, the Council of Economic Advisors, the Central Intelligence Agency, and the Domestic Council — should be subject to Senate confirmation.

---

1. Professor Yarmolinsky states: "I would add statutory appeals procedures, including judicial review."

RECOMMENDATION XXVIII

The senior personal advisors in the White House Office should not be subject to Senate confirmation.

(Adopted overwhelmingly)

Commentary: The Conference was of the opinion that the senior advisors to the President — the Counsellors to the President, his National Security Advisor, his Staff Assistants, his Press Secretary, his speechwriters and similar officials — were personal to him and should not be subject to Senate confirmation.

Dissent from Recommendations
Presidential Powers in Domestic Affairs

Professor Elmer E. Cornwell, Jr. registers disagreement with the overall thrust of the Recommendations in this section of the Final Report. He disagrees with the belief that the American presidency has accumulated too much power in domestic affairs. He states: "If this has happened, it is much more the fault of Congress than the Presidency. The latter has accepted delegation from the legislative branch, and attempted to fill the vacuum left by Congress' inability to formulate overall domestic policy. Moreover, I believe that even if Congress had played a more effective role in the formulation of domestic policy, the role of the President would have to be a major and growing one in light of the complexities of policy making in the late twentieth century."

Professor Mayhew reserves judgment on Presidential Powers in Domestic Affairs. In particular, he has reservations about some conclusions in the Summary and also, specifically, Recommendation XX.

PRESIDENTIAL WAR POWERS

by Professor Raoul Berger
Charles Warren Senior Fellow
in American Legal History
Harvard Law School

Passage of the War Powers Resolution of 1973[1] over the veto of President Nixon marked the end of an era: henceforth unilateral war-making by the President would not go unchallenged. The Resolution premised that there are constitutional metes and bounds to war-making by the President; and it signalled that Congress meant to resume its place in the sun. Watergate served to hammer home the lesson of Vietnam — presidential disregard of constitutional limits threatens our democratic system.

"War," said James Madison, is "the true nurse of executive aggrandizement";[2] one needs only to study the extraordinary expansion of presidential power during the Wilson and Roosevelt regimes in World Wars I and II[3] to appreciate the force of that apothegm. During the post-World War II years, presidential aggrandizement in no small part was nourished by congressional acquiescence, itself a reaction to the consequences of pre-war neutralism and appeasement which had facilitated Fascist and Nazi aggression. Given also the air of sustained crisis engendered by the post-war territorial expansion of Soviet communism, and our own crusading zeal to contain it, to become as it were an international policeman, it is not surprising that Congress and the people, still under the spell of Franklin Roosevelt's leadership, should look to an all-wise President for counter-measures and solutions. The scholarly literature of the period exalts the presidential role; when Senator Robert Taft warned that Truman's unilateral commitment of troops to the Korean conflict lacked constitutional warrant,[4] he was excoriated by leading scholars. As a result, those who later attacked the subsequent Johnson-Nixon commitment in Vietnam were open to the charge of employing a double standard, turning on whose ox was gored.

Self-evidently the Constitution cannot thus change color according to whether at any given time presidential actions coincide with the value judgments of its critics.[5] Since I was among the critics

of the Johnson-Nixon policy, I may be permitted to say that as long ago as 1942 I wrote that I liked it no better when the Court read *my* predilections into the Constitution than when McReynolds, Butler & Co. read in theirs.[6] We cannot afford to allow any power structure to treat the Constitution as an accordion which it can expand or contract at will.

But why, it has been asked, should a nation of 200 million people be held in thrall by a document that was framed for a little seaboard folk of 3 million; why should it be enslaved by "the words of the Constitution as timeless absolutes?"[7] That question poses a false issue. The Constitution itself provides for change by the process of amendment. What those who would not be enslaved by "the words of the Constitution" seek is to take away from the people the decision they have reserved to themselves. Upon the plea that the amendment process is too cumbersome, the servants and agents of the people would informally amend the Constitution without consulting them. Ours, however, is a government by consent of the governed. The people, said James Iredell, later a Justice of the Supreme Court, "have chosen to be governed under such and such principles. They have not chosen to be governed or promised to submit upon any other."[8] The arch-activist, Justice Hugo Black, rejected the notion that in order "to keep the Constitution in tune with the times" it "must be changed from time to time and that this Court is charged with a duty to make those changes . . . The Constitution makers knew the need for change and provided for it."[9] All the less can the President be allowed single-handedly to revise the Constitution and reallocate to himself powers granted to Congress and deliberately withheld from him. The Framers justly feared the insatiable greed for power of those entrusted with office and sought to curb it by a careful distribution, enumeration, and limitation of powers. It needs no recital of Richard Nixon's excesses to remind us that the exercise of power must be confined within the terms of the original grant lest violations of these limits threaten the liberties of all.

A further preliminary word about the allegedly "enigmatic" quality of the constitutional materials. Such expressions rely on a statement by Justice Jackson in the "Steel Seizure Case."[10] Notwithstanding, Jackson experienced no difficulty in finding the original intention clear enough to lead him emphatically to reject inflated presidential claims of war powers. Others have stressed the inadequacy of the constitutional records. On the subject of war, however, there is crystal-clear confirmation by prominent delegates to the Convention, by *The Federalist,* and in the several Ratification Conventions. And, as will appear, the face of the Constitution speaks clearly enough to those who will but listen.

Repeatedly we are admonished not to dismantle or cut back the powers of the presidency.[11] Such comments mistake the thrust of the War Powers Resolution, which sought rather to restore the original constitutional distribution of powers. The problem is not one of *abuse* of granted powers[12] by the President but rather of *usurpation* of powers unmistakably granted to the Congress and withheld from him. For the Founders, usurpation of powers — subversion of the Constitution — was the cardinal impeachable offence.[13]

Adoption by Congress of the War Powers Resolution could not, of course, settle the constitutional issue. In vetoing the measure, President Nixon labeled it unconstitutional, following the view earlier expressed by Secretary of State William Rogers. Professor Eugene Rostow also regarded it as a "serious attack on the Constitution" which "would destroy the Presidency" and "abolish the principle of the separation of powers."[14] Such doubts continue to be voiced,[15] and it is fitting that we should here attempt to clarify the issue for the benefit of the American people.

This is likewise a fitting occasion to recall the words of the 1780 Massachusetts Constitution, drafted by John Adams:

A frequent recurrence to the fundamental principles of the constitution. . .[is] absolutely necessary to preserve the advantages of liberty and to maintain a free government. The people . . . have a right to require of their lawgivers and magistrates an exact and constant observance of them.[16]

The starting point for any discussion of the location of the war-making power should be the constitutional text. As the great English advocate, later Lord Chancellor, Thomas Erskine said of a statute in one of the State trials, the Constitution is "ever present to speak for itself."[17] So too, we must look at the Constitution with eyes unclouded by the opinion of others.

But first a few words should be said about the historical background from which the Constitution emerged. Among the Colonists, the prevalent belief was that " 'the executive magistracy' was the natural enemy, the legislative assembly the natural friend of liberty."[18] This derived in part from the fact that the House of Commons had been the cradle of liberty in the seventeenth century struggle against Stuart absolutism, a period that greatly influenced Colonial thinking.[19] Then too, Colonial assemblies were elected by the Colonists themselves and enjoyed their trust, whereas governors and judges were saddled on them by the Crown. It resulted that in most of the early State constitutions the governor's office was "reduced almost to the dimensions of a symbol," with all roots in the royal prerogative cut.[20]

When the Colonists assembled in the Continental Congress and adopted the Articles of Confederation, they dispensed with an executive altogether, and gave the Congress "the sole and exclusive right and power of determining on peace and war."[21] Although the early State constitutions had set up an executive, his war-making role, as will appear, was quite circumscribed. A commentator recently concluded that "Out of this national and state experience, there seems to have emerged little if any dissatisfaction with legislative control over decisions to go to war and make peace."[22] Not surprisingly, therefore, the early patterns strongly influenced the Framers, as the face of the Constitution itself attests. Indeed, the draft submitted by the Committee on Detail provided that the legislature should "make war," lifting this as well as other powers granted to the Continental Congress "bodily from the old Articles of Confederation."[23]

The Constitutional text respecting the war powers strikingly exhibits a vast disproportion between those conferred on Congress and on the

President. Three little words—Commander-in-Chief —comprise the sum and substance of the presidential grant; whereas the Congress — but let James Wilson, next to Madison the leading architect of the Constitution, speak:

> The power of declaring war, and the other powers naturally connected with it, are vested in congress. To provide and maintain a navy — to make rules for its government — to grant letters of marque and reprisal — to make rules concerning captures — to raise and support armies — to establish rules for their regulation — to provide for organizing . . . the militia and for calling them forth in the service of the Union — all these are powers naturally connected with the power of declaring war. All these powers, therefore, are vested in Congress.[24]

To this may be added that Congress is also empowered to "provide for the common Defence" and to make appropriations for the foregoing purposes.

Since all the powers "naturally connected" with that of declaring war are vested in Congress, it follows that they are not to be exercised by the President. The President, said Wilson, "is to take care that the laws be faithfully executed; he is commander in chief of the army and navy."[25] How narrowly the function was conceived may be gathered from the fact that in appointing George Washington as Commander-in-Chief, the Continental Congress made sure, as Professor Rostow said, that he was to be "its creature . . . in every respect."[26] Virtually every early State Constitution framed prior to the Federal Convention made the Governor commander-in-chief, to act under the laws of the State, that is to say, subject to governance by the legislature.[27] The Convention adopted the words "Commander-in-Chief" without explanation; those who would give them a broader meaning than they had for the Continental Congress and the States carry the burden of proof that such was the intention of the Framers.[28] No such evidence exists. Instead, Hamilton explained in *The Federalist* that the President's powers were less than those of some State governors,[29] that as Commander-in-Chief his authority "would amount to nothing more than the supreme command and direction of the military and naval forces, as first General and admiral. . ."[30]

"[G]enerals and admirals," Professor Louis Henkin reminds us, "even when they are 'first' do not determine the political purposes for which troops are to be used; they command them in the execution of policy made by others."[31] The records of the Convention make plain that it was not for the President to "begin" or "commence" a war, but only to "conduct" it when authorized by Congress, or when begun by invasion of the United States.[32] All appeals to the "Commander-in-Chief" phrase must therefore proceed from the incontrovertible fact that the Framers designed the role merely for command of the armed forces as "first general and admiral."

This distribution of powers was not inadvertent; the severely limited role of the President was a studied response to what Madison termed an axiom, the "axiom that the executive is . . . most distinguished by its propensity to war: hence it is the practice [in free states] to disarm this propensity . . . ." The object, in Wilson's homespun phrase, was to prevent a "single man" from "hurrying" us into war, a lesson we have had to relearn at bitter cost in Vietnam.[33]

A powerful summation of the Framers' intention was made in 1793 by Madison:

> Every just view that can be taken of the subject, admonishes the public of the necessity of a rigid adherence to the simple, the received, and the fundamental doctrine of the constitution, that the power to declare war, including the *power of judging the causes of war*, is fully and exclusively vested in the legislature; that the executive has no right *in any case*, to decide the question, whether there is or is not cause for declaring war; that the right of convening and informing congress, whenever such a question seems to call for a decision, *is all the right* which the constitution has deemed requisite or proper.[34]

On this score, there was little difference between Madison and Hamilton; even after Hamilton had moved from a narrow to a broader view of executive power, he still declared that it is the

> exclusive province of Congress, *when the nation is at peace,* to change that state into a state of war . . . *it belongs to Congress only, to go to war.*[35]

Presidential authority to defend against invasion is not expressly conferred upon the President as it is upon the States; it is drawn from a proposal by Madison and Gerry to leave to the President power "to repel sudden attack," plainly reflecting Roger Sherman's view that the "Executive shd. be able to repel and not to commence war."[36] This was a limited *grant* to the President when, as the words "sudden attack" imply, there would be no time to consult with Congress.[37] And there is good reason to believe that it was an attack upon the territory of the United States that was contemplated. The antecedent Articles of Confederation had authorized a State to resist invasion of its own soil; authority did not extend to invasion of a contiguous State in the "league of friendship." Georgia was not authorized to resist invasion of New York, much less of Canada. And the authority was spelled out in terms of "actual" invasion of "such state" or danger "so imminent as not to admit of a delay, till the united states in congress assembled can be consulted."[38] A similar provision was embodied in Article I, §10(3) of the Constitution. Thus, the Framers well understood the difference between actual invasion and imminent threat of invasion, and they expressly empowered a State to meet both. No mention whatever was made, in any of the Conventions, of a presidential power to react to such imminent danger, and the omission is the more significant against the background of strictly enumerated powers and pervasive jealousy of executive power. To be sure, there must be a means of meeting a Cuban missiles crisis, but the path lies by Congressional authorization. Against this background, talk of a "pattern of shared Constitutional authority"[39] recalls the tale about the little tailor who slew seven flies at a stroke and sallied forth wearing the motto "seven at a blow." Duly impressed, a towering giant acceded to his suggested test of the tailor's prowess, that they share in carrying a huge felled tree; the giant to carry the trunk, the tailor the branches.[40]

From time to time it is sought to strengthen the case for the President by appeal to his "inherent" powers, to the "Executive Power," to the Founders' design to create a "strong" presidency. Following the view expressed by Hamilton in 1793, Chief Justice Taft stressed the difference between the grant to Congress of "all legislative powers herein granted" and the Article II phrase "The executive Power shall be vested in a President . . . ."[40a] Viewed alone, this difference might suggest an intention to create an unlimited executive, in contrast to a limited legislative, power. Madison stated, however, that the "executive power [was] restrained within a narrower compass" than the legislative.[41] The language variation is a result of drafting changes to solve the problem of a single versus a multiple President.[42] Undeniably the Convention moved to a "strong executive," but to one of enumerated functions. Emphasis upon the effect of enumeration is frequently met. Governor Randolph, defending the Constitution in the Virginia Ratification Convention, said that the powers of government

> are enumerated. Is it not, then fairly deducible that it has no power but what is expressly given it? – for if its powers were to be general, an enumeration would be needless.[43]

In the North Carolina Convention, James Iredell stated, "It is necessary to particularize the powers intended to be given . . . but, after having enumerated what we give up, it follows . . . that whatever is done by virtue of that authority is legal."[44] Conversely, lacking an "enumerated" power, action is illegal.

The President, too, was to be governed by particularization. From the beginning, it was emphasized that executive powers must be enumerated "to assist the judgment how far they might be safely entrusted to a single officer."[45] Madison stated the matter with unmistakable clarity: preliminarily it was essential "to *fix the extent* of the Executive authority . . . as certain powers were in their nature executive, and *must be given* to that departmnt. . . ." The executive powers, he said "shd. be confined and defined,"[46] as they later were in the sparse enumeration of executive powers.

Reliance upon generalizations about a "strong President" falls afoul of such utterances as that of Charles Pinckney in the Federal Convention; he

> was for a vigorous Executive, but was afraid the Executive powers . . . might extend to peace & war etc. which would render the Executive a Monarch, of the worst kind . . . ."[47]

The leader of the "strong executive party," James Wilson, said that the "only powers he conceived strictly Executive were those of executing the laws and appointing officers."[48] In truth, it is incongruous to attribute to a generation so in dread of executive tyranny an intention to give a newly created executive a blank check,[49] and this at the very moment when it was cautiously enumerating the powers that were being granted, down to the veriest trifle — the express authorization to "require the Opinion in writing" of each department head which, as Justice Jackson remarked. "would seem to be inherent in the Executive if anything is."[50] And the argument of "inherent" executive power flies in the face of Madison's statement in *The Federalist* that the "executive magistracy is carefully limited, both in the extent and the duration of its power."[51] It was flatly rejected by Justice Jackson in the "Steel Seizure Case,"[52] and it remains to be said on this score that Justices Holmes and Brandeis dissented from the view of Chief Justice Taft, and their view was later adopted by Justices Black, Douglas, Frankfurter and Jackson.[53]

The Executive department, so far as I can find, has never disputed the foregoing view of the "original intention." Indeed it was tacitly conceded in 1966 by the Legal Advisor of the State Department:

In 1787 the world was a far larger place, and the framers probably had in mind attacks upon the United States In the 20th century the world has grown much smaller. An attack on a country far from our shores can impinge directly on the nation's security . . . The Constitution leaves to the President the judgment to determine whether the circumstances of a particular armed attack are so urgent and the potential consequences so threatening to the security of the United States that he should act without formally consulting the Congress.[54]

Presumably, this was a reference to the Commander-in-Chief power, for no other power, save for repulsion of sudden attack on the United States, is conferred on the President. Only in that exceptional instance might he act without consulting Congress. There is no constitutional doctrine that presidential power increases in inverse proportion to shrinkage of the world.

When Secretary of State Acheson opined that President Truman was empowered to commit troops to repel the sudden invasion of Korea, he relied on the President's "constitutional authority as Commander in Chief." Without taking account of the "original intention," he later explained that "The basis for this conclusion" was a State Department memorandum of 1950 which "listed eighty-seven instances in the past century in which [Truman's] predecessors" had exercised "presidential power to send our forces into battle."[55] These incidents, since greatly increased in number, have been analyzed in detail by Professors Wormuth, Schlesinger and others,[56] and do not call for still another going-over. The "vast majority" of such cases, said Corwin, "involved fights with pirates, landings of small naval contingents on barbarous or semi-barbarous coasts [to protect American citizens], the dispatch of small bodies of troops to chase bandits or cattle rustlers across the Mexican border."[57] Prior to Korea, the high-water mark was reached by the shipment of 5,000 troops to Peking to concert with English, French and German forces in the protection of their nationals from the rebellious Boxer forces.[58] These incidents, it is to be noted, did not involve nations capable of resisting such incursions but situations where the possibility of war was remote, far removed from "send[ing] our forces into battle." As Corwin noted, they were defended "as not amounting to acts of war."[59] And their professed basis, protection of American citizens, is constitutionally questionable. Secretary of State Rogers acknowledged in 1971 that "The origin of the notion . . . that citizens have a right to protection abroad is unclear."[60] Whatever the origin of the citizen's right, President Buchanan recognized that the protective power resided in Congress:

I deem it my duty once more earnestly to recommend to Congress the passage of a law authorizing the President to employ the naval force . . . for the purpose of protecting the lives and property of American citizens passing in transit across the Panama . . . routes.[61]

Abandoning Acheson's far-fetched claims, Rogers testified that the "historical [presidential] precedents" are not "dispositive of the constitutional issues," and "disavowed them as a precedent."[62] Give these "precedents" their widest scope and it is yet an astronomical jump from the 5,000 troops sent to Peking to the 500,000 troops committed to sustained warfare in Vietnam at a cost of 45,000 dead and 200,000 maimed and wounded.

In the context of executive agreements, Professor Myres McDougal argued that "continuance of [a] practice by successive administrations throughout our history makes its contemporary constitutionality unquestionable."[63] This may be well enough when no more is involved than construction of amorphous powers granted to the President. But the case stands differently when it is sought to justify presidential reallocation to himself of power exclusively granted to Congress. Usurpation of power is not legitimated by repetition. So the Supreme Court has held.[64] The President can no more take over powers conferred by the Constitution on Congress through a long course of practice than he can revise the Constitution by a stroke of the pen. "An agent cannot new model his own commission," said Hamilton.[65] If this generation has not learned from President Nixon that such claims imperil our democratic society, it is unteachable.

Professor Rostow's Critique

The attempt by the War Powers Bill to restore the constitutional balance was stamped by Professor Eugene Rostow as a "serious attack on the Constitution," which "would destroy the Presidency" and abolish . . . the separation of powers."[66] Though he was constrained at length to concede that "no one contests" that "Congress has the exclusive power to authorize a state of war,"[67] he maintained that the Bill "would be an unconstitutional interference with the President's inherent power to conduct our foreign relations, and to interpret and apply our treaty obligations in the first instance."[68]

But let me begin at the beginning. Rostow notices that my views of the "original intention" are shared by Professors Charles A. Lofgren, William Van Alstyne and Francis D. Wormuth.[69] But without discussing our evidence, he downgrades our meticulous recital of the facts of record as our "version of the Constitution," bare "hypotheses."[70] He allows that "much can be said of [our] related *theories* . . . as *formulations* of the original intent of the Founding Fathers."[71] But these "theories" are said to founder on one fact, "a fact which conclusively disproves all [our] hypotheses at once: The treaty power, and the Founding Fathers' intimate experience with that power in connection

with the Benjamin Franklin Treaties with France of 1778." In short, he defends the Korean and Vietnam conflicts as "fought under the authority of treaties."[72]

His discussion jumps off from Van Alstyne's statement that a congressional transfer of authority to the President to embark upon war

> cannot be accomplished by *treaty*. The House of Representatives prerequisite consent to this nation's involvement in war was most deliberately required by the declaration of war clause after consideration of several alternatives, including the specific proposed alternative of vesting the power jointly in the Senate and President alone which was itself rejected. As the House does not consent to treaties, manifestly a treaty cannot be among the possible means of delegating its authority. To imply that the constitutional draftsmen could possibly have formulated a document so specific in its precautions against involvements in war while simultaneously creating an enormous loophole of exclusive Senate power to give it away by simple treaty ratification is wholly without logic or evidence.[73]

To my mind this is incontrovertible. Rostow himself states that "Van Alstyne's argument is perfectly logical. But, like so many logical arguments, it i[s] destroyed by a page of history."[74] Rostow's page of history, alas, turns out to be an appeal to fantasy.

The Franklin Treaty of Alliance with Franc[e] of 1778 contained an "American guarantee of 'th[e] present possessions of the Crown of France i[n] America.' "[75] Mark that this was a treaty entere[d] into by the unicameral Continental Congress, i[n] which resided plenary power to determine on wa[r] and peace, and, therefore, it sheds no light o[n] whether the Senate alone can commit the nation t[o] war without the concurrence of the House. Th[is] treaty, regarded by the Founders, states Rostow[,] with "reverence as a pillar of the Nation's exis[]tence,"[76] did not prompt President Washington t[o] come to the aid of France in its war with Britai[n.] Quite the contrary; Washington "issued a proclama[]tion of neutrality."[77] Such was the "Foundin[g] Fathers' intimate experience with that power i[n] connection with the Benjamin Frankl[in] Treaties . . . "; instead of a "page of history[,]

Rostow pulled a blank. So he resorts to speculation: "Suppose [Washington] had put garrisons and naval forces in the French Islands of the Caribbean," French possessions that the Treaty bound us to "guarantee." "Suppose," too, that Washington "had convoyed vessels to those islands, and repelled British attacks on the vessels, or on the islands. Would it be possible to say . . . that the President could not respond to such 'sudden' attacks exactly as if they were 'sudden' attacks upon the United States?"[78] Thus Rostow puts Washington's neck into a noose that he carefully avoided, and asks us to decide a grave constitutional issue on the basis of imaginary facts, a decision the Supreme Court almost never undertakes. His pervasive mistake is to assume that because there is a necessity for the nation to act, it necessarily follows that the President must implicitly be empowered to do so. But as Justice Frankfurter stated, the fact "that power exists in the Government does not vest it in the President."[79]

Although the Framers preserved subsisting treaties, they did not place them above the Constitution.[80] Having so carefully put it beyond the power of a "single man," in James Wilson's words, to "hurry" us into war, when the Framers were focussing squarely on the distribution of the war powers, they scarcely intended by their ratification of the 1778 treaty to throw these labors into the discard. Rather, the reasonable presumption is that they meant execution of the treaty to be subject to the constitutional provisions respecting the power to wage war. To the extent that effectuation of the "guarantee" to France entailed war-making, the Constitution left the decision to Congress. If the history of the Franklin treaty teaches anything, it is that, far from encouraging the President to adventure into war on his own, Washington felt free to violate the treaty when war actually threatened to embroil the nation. Would that his successors had exhibited equal wisdom in Korea and Vietnam.

Rostow picks up the argument by invoking post-World War II treaties which provide that "an armed attack against one or more of the allies shall be considered an attack against them all. That declaration flies in the face of the supposed constitutional principle Mr. Berger and others find in the original intent of the Founding Fathers. Their version of the Constitution would confine the President's emergency powers to attacks on the territory of the United States. Either the treaty is unconstitutional or their version of the original intent is inadequate and erroneous."[81] These are false alternatives because the treaties carefully safeguarded the congressional war-making prerogative. In a colloquy with Secretary of State Dulles, Chairman Alexander Wiley of the Senate Foreign Relations Committee, asked respecting one such provision with reference to

> meeting the common danger. Would it be in accord with the constitutional processes?
> Secretary Dulles. Yes Sir.
> The Chairman. So whether it were the threat mentioned in section 2 or the common danger resulting from open attack, action could be taken only after consultation with Congress.
> Secretary Dulles. Yes Sir.[82]

Rostow comments that both Wiley and Dulles "carefully avoided the view that we could act . . . after only a congressional declaration of limited or unlimited war. Consultation is an elastic process, which can and does occur at breakfasts. . . ."[83] It was precisely such free and easy interpretations that led the State Department to encourage presidential war-making. But Wiley, of course, assimilated "consultation" with his immediately preceding reference to "constitutional processes." Whatever may have been Dulles' unuttered notions of the meaning *he* attached to those processes, Wiley left no doubt as to his own understanding.

The heart of the relevant article 4(1), in Dulles' words, "The agreement of each of the parties to meet the common danger ["aggression by means of armed attack"] 'in accordance with its constitutional processes' . . ." is duplicated in the treaty with Korea,[84] which was discussed in the Senate debates by Chairman Wiley. In response to questions by Senators John Stennis and Arthur Watkins, Wiley stated,

> There is no question in my mind that the phrase 'constitutional processes' means action by Congress. I have said so 3 or 4 times in different ways . . .

Senator Watkins asked, "Congress would have to make the decision whether the United States would go to war or would not go to war?" Wiley replied, "The Senator is correct." The record is studded with such remarks by Wiley.[85] Senator Smith, on whom Rostow relies for the "Monroe Doctrine approach," stated that in case of a violation of the Monroe Doctrine in South America, "The President should be prepared to issue a stern warning and have Congress back of him and ask for the support of Congress." He "absolutely agreed" with Senator Watkins that before the President "ordered out the Armed Forces . . . the President by all means should come to Congress and get power to take that action."[86] Commentators justifiably take that view of "constitutional processes," and it is based on unassailable reason.[87] No treaty rises higher than the Constitution;[88] and it was precisely for that reason that the words "constitutional processes" were inserted into the treaties and designed to insure the participation of the House in any authorization to make war,[89] and to put foreign nations on notice of the fact.

Professor Rostow also quoted at length from Hamilton's "Pacificus" papers of 1793, wherein he enunciated the novel theory that the Executive was given plenary power by the words "Executive power," not confined to the subsequent enumeration of powers; and that the congressional war powers and Senate participation in the treaty power were "exceptions" which must be strictly construed.[90] His views on the effect of the enumeration, as we have seen, cannot stand up in the face of the historical record.[91] And they represent a *volte face,* a repudiation of assurances he had made in *The Federalist* to procure adoption of the Constitution.[92] Madison, replying under the nom-de-plume "Helvidius," nailed this repudiation to the mast. According to John Quincy Adams, Madison "scrutinized the doctrines of Pacificus with an acuteness of intellect never perhaps surpassed"; his "most forcible arguments are pointed with quotations from the papers of *The Federalist* written by Hamilton."[93] Nevertheless, Rostow agrees with Professor Corwin that "Hamilton's view has prevailed."[94] It is true that Corwin stated, "history has awarded the palm of victory to Pacificus," meaning that "[b]y his reading of the 'executive power' clause 'Pacificus' gave the President constitutional warrant to go ahead and apply the advantages of his position in a field of power to which they are specially adapted."[95] That "Pacificus" views were congenial to presidential expansionism is hardly deniable; but whether they

afford a "constitutional warrant" must turn on the validity of his arguments rather than their subsequent adoption by Presidents whose purposes they served. Rostow overlooked Corwin's statement that the "story as a whole only emphasizes the essential truth of 'Helvidius' ' contention that 'Pacificus' ' reading of the executive power clause contravened, certainly in effect, the express intention of the Constitution that the war-declaring power should lodge with legislative authority."[96] Since Corwin wrote, the Supreme Court, in the "Steel Seizure Case," rejected the presidential claim to a reservoir of power and rebuffed President Truman's invasion of Congressional prerogative.[97] Thereby it acted in harmony with the historical record, not with "Pacificus." Our task here, I take it, is to look at that record rather than later shifting statements by Hamilton about it.[98]

We should not take our leave of Professor Rostow without taking note of his warning against confining "the President's emergency powers."[99] In Justice Jackson's opinion in the "Steel Seizure Case," what Rostow considers as "probably his finest opinion,"[100] Jackson stated,

The appeal . . . that we declare the existence of inherent powers *ex necessitate* to meet an emergency asks us to do . . . something the forefathers omitted. They knew what emergencies were, knew the pressures they engender for authoritative action, knew, too, how they afford a ready pretext for usurpation. . . Aside from suspension of the privilege of the writ of habeas corpus in time of rebellion or invasion . . . they made no provision for exercise of extraordinary authority because of a crisis. I do not think that we rightfully may so amend their work.

Emergency powers, Jackson continued,

are consistent with free government only when their control is lodged elsewhere than in the Executive who exercises them. That is the safeguard that would be nullified by our adoption of the "inherent powers" formula.[101]

Not the least curious challenge to the constitutionality of the War Powers Resolution comes from Senator Howard Baker, now regarded as potential Republican candidate for President. In October, 1973, Senator Baker stated that th authority conferred on Congress by the War Powers Bill "diminish[ed] what would appear to be the authority given to the President by Article IV, Section 4. That, I am sure will be thrashed out in the courts someday."[102] Article IV, §4 provides that "The United States shall ... protect each [State] against invasion." Assume that this power is lodged in the President and it is yet a narrow power, to protect against invasion of the territory of a State, e.g. Georgia, not a warrant to invade Korea. Moreover, it is given *to Congress* by Article I, §8(15) "To provide for *calling* forth the militia ... repel invasions," while Article II, §2(1) merely provides that "The President shall be Commander-in-Chief of the militia ... *when called* to the actual service of the United States."[103] Thus, the power conferred on the President is subject to congressional control. Unless Congress provides for calling out the militia, no power exists in the President to employ it.

The starting point must ever be the fact that the Constitution reserves war-making to Congress, save for the authority of the Commander-in-Chief to repel an attack upon the United States or its territories. To Congress is given the power to "declare" war, and as the constitutional records show and Justice Story stated, "A power to declare war is a power to make and carry on war."[104] The difficulties in which Congress became enmeshed in framing the War Powers Resolution in 1973 largely derive from the reluctance of some of its members to come to grips with this fact. It may be that many have been brain-washed by the incessant presidential propaganda for independent war-making powers and have not taken pains to inquire into the historical unreliability of such representations. It may be, too, that many members of Congress shrink from assuming responsibility for the tremendous decisions involved. Section 2 of the Resolution represents an attempt by Congress to return to the constitutional design, so severely disrupted by the Nixon administration, by formally setting forth its understanding of the constitutional perimeters of the Commander-in-Chief function: except for attack upon the United States or its armed forces, the President must seek congressional authorization to commence war.

To the extent that it is thought essential to broaden the President's power to meet modern exigencies, that can be done by Congressional delegation. The Framers, we have seen, differentiated between the presidential power to repel an *actual* attack upon the United States and that of the States to act in the face of an *imminent danger* of attack. What about presidential authority to meet nuclear attacks? Nuclear attack means, I take it, the actual dropping of missiles on the United States, its territories or its armed forces. There is no way of knowing when a thumb will press the button in Moscow; hence, presidential response must be triggered by falling missiles. If the President is to *initiate* nuclear warfare, that entails a departure from the announced policy of retaliatory bombing. So grave is that departure as to call for congressional approval *before* the President presses the nuclear button. It is hard to conceive a situation where that initiative cannot be put before a secret session of Congress or, at the very least, to the leadership and appropriate committees of Congress.

Danger of "imminent" attack is better illustrated by the sneak attack on Pearl Harbor. Suppose that once more a foreign flotilla and planes are sighted several hundred miles from our shores, posing the danger of "imminent" attack. A delegation of power to meet that danger is plainly required. The difficulty with the earlier Javits formula "to forestall the direct and imminent threat" of attack upon the United States or upon its armed forces "located outside the United States" was that it was overbroad.[105] A statutory formula must avoid the danger perceived by Lincoln in 1842, the danger that the President can, if he thinks necessary, invade Canada or Mexico to prevent an anticipated invasion by them.[106] There, some form of prior congressional control seems indispensable, particularly if he would send troops to Siberia to prevent the "imminent" danger of invasion of the United States. To deal with attacks upon the armed forces "located outside the United States" requires some congressional control over deployment, a matter hereinafter considered. Congress cannot escape the problem by determining to let the President act on his own without congressional authorization. That would be to shut its eyes to an unconstitutional exercise of powers that the Constitution confided to Congress, an abdication of congressional responsibility. For that reason, I dissent from Senator J. W. Fulbright's suggestion that the President should be left free to act on his own responsibility, to be called to account after the fact by Congress.[107] Such accountings cannot restore needlessly lost lives or extricate us from unwanted wars.

It has been objected that the restrictive enumeration of authorized presidential initiatives would have prevented President Franklin Roosevelt from taking some of his steps to keep Great Britain afloat before Pearl Harbor.[108] This is not the place to assess the constitutionality of Roosevelt's pre-Pearl Harbor actions. On the assumption that they fell outside the powers of a "first General," and that restrictions such as §2(c) expresses are merely declarative of the Constitution's war-making provisions, we must not bend the Constitution to conform to our predilections. Those who approved of Truman's intervention in Korea and later disapproved of the Johnson-Nixon involvement in Vietnam, came to see that judgment must turn on disinterested search for constitutional meaning and even-handed application of that meaning, let the chips fall where they may. The fact that renewal of the draft in 1941 was carried by only one vote in the House of Representatives indicates that the nation was divided.[109] The "power of declaring war," in the words of Justice Story, is "so critical and calamitous, that [it requires] the utmost deliberation, and the successive review of all the councils of the nation."[110]

A nation which must be saved in spite of itself, whose salvation must depend upon the determination of a single man — today Franklin Roosevelt, tomorrow Nixon — is in parlous straits —"Unhappy the land that needs a hero."[111] Roosevelt, it needs always to be remembered, stopped short of war, and turned to Congress for a declaration of war after Pearl Harbor had united the nation. "Vietnam has shown us," said war hawk Senator John Stennis, "that by trying to fight a war without the clear-cut prior support of the American people we ... strain, and can shatter the very structure of the Republic."[112] On the whole, the hypothetical costs of insisting on prior congressional approval, it seems to me, are outweighed by the actual costs of embarking on adventures such as Korea and Vietnam without congressional debate. To be sure, there have been times when it was Congress that pressed for war; and there may again

be instances when congressional wisdom falls short. But presidential folly also has cost us dearly. If power is vested in Congress by the Constitution, it is not to be reallocated to the President on the ground that Congress may be unwise. For me, the paramount consideration is observance of constitutional limits. When we countenance the President's allocation to himself of powers withheld from him, the entire democratic structure is endangered.

Delegation to the President

Professor Francis Wormuth, who performed yeoman service in piercing presidential pretensions to independent war-making power,[113] argues against prior delegations and urges that congressional decision for war-making must be taken contemporaneously with the declaration of war.[114] This is the highest desideratum; but there may be danger so imminent as to leave no time for consultation. The Constitution, in my judgment, does not preclude delegations to meet such contingencies. First, having concluded that plenary war-making power was vested in Congress rather than the President, I would be guided by Marshall's statement in *McCulloch v. Maryland*:

> It must have been the intention of those who gave these powers, to insure ... their beneficial execution. This could not be done by confining the choice of means to such narrow limits as not to leave it in the power of Congress to adopt any which might be appropriate, and which were conducive to the end.[115]

Second, the historical course of Congress, charted in part by Professor Wormuth, is not all one way. It will be recalled that Article I, §8(15) empowered Congress "To provide for calling forth the Militia ... to repel Invasion." Instead of providing detailed expression of policy, Congress authorized the President by the Act of 1795 to call forth the militia "whenever the United States shall be invaded, or be in imminent danger of invasion,"[116] following a pattern set out in the Constitution itself.

Like Professor Wormuth, I little relish congressional issuance of a blank check to determine policy; and I am aware that, on the domestic front, it was said in *Panama Refining Co. v. Ryan* that Congress must establish a "criterion to govern the President's course."[117] A criterion, however, can only be made as explicit as the particular circumstances permit; and the fact that the Framers themselves employed a formula hardly more specific— the Article I, §10(3) authorization to a State to engage in war if "in such imminent danger as will not admit of delay" — persuades that statutory criteria framed in similar terms are not unduly broad. In fine, the limits on delegation must not be so rigorously applied as to render *both* Congress and the President powerless to cope with the fearful exigencies of our contemporary world. Whatever the limits on congressional delegation, here they must yield to the overriding need perceived by Hamilton:

> The circumstances that endanger the safety of nations are infinite, and for this reason no constitutional shackles can wisely be imposed on the power to which the care of it is committed.[118]

This is not to be read as freeing the President from limits imposed by the Constitution, but to allow Congress, to which the power was "committed," to delegate power to the President to meet "imminent danger" to the nation. It is no easy matter to frame standards that will anticipate the myriad unpredictable circumstances that, in future, will authorize the President unilaterally to commit our forces to battle. But the alternative cannot be that he must be left at large, for that is constitutionally impermissible. Congressional foresight will fall short of perfection, but the attempt to frame a limited authorization can go a long way to warn the President against excesses. And it may serve as a basis for an appeal to the courts, a matter to which I shall recur.

Deployment and Congressional Control

Without congressional control over deployment of our armed forces outside the United States, legislative limitations on presidential authorizations to repel attacks on such forces are virtually useless. Unless Congress asserts control over deployment by statute requiring congressional authorization, the President will in the future, as in the past, station armed forces in trouble spots where they invite attack. Once such attack occurs, retaliation becomes almost impossible to resist and Congress is faced with a *fait accompli*.

Secretary of State Dean Acheson asserted, however, that: Not only has the President the authority to use the Armed Forces in carrying out the broad foreign policy of the United States and implementing treaties, but it is equally clear that this authority may not be interfered with by Congress in the exercise of powers which it has under the Constitution.[119]

He supplied no reasoning or citation for this sweeping claim, and it can readily be shown that it will not stand up. It is Congress that is to "provide for the common Defence,"[120] which implies the right to decide what is requisite thereto. Congress also is "to raise and support Armies" and, by necessary implication, it can withhold or withdraw that support.[121] In determining the size of the army it will "support," it is entitled to weigh priorities: shall troops be stationed in Germany or deployed in Cambodia? The constitutional mandate that "no appropriation" for support of the armies "shall be for a longer Term than two Years" implies that it is for Congress to decide at any point whether further appropriations should be made and in what amounts.[122] The duty of Congress, in Hamilton's words, "to determine upon the propriety of keeping a military force on foot,"[123] surely comprehends the right to insist that a portion of the military forces should not be kept "on foot" in Vietnam or Europe.

With the power of appropriation goes the right to specify how appropriated moneys shall be spent. This is not a mere matter of logic, but of established parliamentary practice. After 1665, states Hallam, it became "an undisputed principle" that moneys "granted by Parliament, are only to be expended for particular objects specified by itself."[124] The Act of Settlement (1701), for example, provided that appropriations were to be applied "to the several Uses and Purposes by this act directed and intended as aforesaid, and to no other Use, Intent or Purpose whatsoever."[125] The Founders were quite familiar with the parliamentary practice; and we may be sure that, in reposing in Congress the power of raising revenues and reviewing appropriations for support of the armies, they conferred the concomitant right to "specify" the "particular objects" upon which its appropriations are to be expended. So an early Congress read its constitutional powers in enacting a statute that all "sums appropriated by law for each branch of expenditure in the several departments shall be solely applied to the objects for which they are respectively appropriated."[126] The 1971 Act, which prohibits the use of appropriated funds "to finance the introduction of United States ground combat troops into Cambodia," is in this tradition.[127] Such statutes do not constitute an invasion of the President's powers as Commander-in-Chief.

Then there is the congressional power "to make rules for the government and regulation of the land and naval forces."[128] This was "added from the existing Articles of Confederation" but the Framers omitted the phrase that followed —"and directing their operations" — having in mind that the President would be Commander-in-Chief and, in the words of the New Jersey Plan, would "direct all military operations."[129] Thus, the Framers separated the presidential direction of "military operations" in time of war from congressional power to make rules "for the government and regulation of the armed forces," a plenary power enjoyed by the Continental Congress and conferred in identical terms upon the federal Congress. The word "government" connotes a power "to control," "to administer the government" of the armed forces; the word "regulate" means "to dispose, order, or govern." Those powers manifestly embrace congressional restraint upon deployment of the armed forces. Historically, it has been noted, the power of a Commander-in-Chief was exceedingly limited. Washington was expressly made subject to the direction of the Continental Congress; and in early State constitutions the functions of the Governor as Commander-in-Chief was made subject to law, *i.e.* to the legislature, a corollary of the "received opinion" that war-making was the function of the legislature, not of the "first General." There is no inkling in the several Convention records of an intent to confer a broader power on the President; to the contrary, it was on several occasions pointed out that his powers were no broader than those of State governors. In fine, the constitutional distribution of powers refutes Acheson's assumption that the President may deploy the armed forces in disregard of the congressional will.[130]

The questions presented by congressional control over deployment are, therefore, questions of policy, not of constitutional power. Some light may be gathered from the past. When President Truman proposed in 1951 to send four additional divisio[ns] to Europe, he gave rise to a debate, the upshot [of] which was a "sense of the Senate" resolution th[at] approved "the sending of the divisions but adde[d] over administration opposition, that no additiona[l] ground troops should be sent . . . 'without furth[er] congressional approval.' "[131] Of Presiden[t] Kennedy's shipment of 15,000 troops to Vietna[m] Professor Bickel remarked that "you would have [to] be very disingenuous not to have thought you we[re] throwing them into a place where there was a thre[at] of hostilities."[132] The nation would have bee[n] better off had Congress debated that deploymen[t.] On the other hand, a deployment of an addition[al] 1,000 troops to a non-trouble spot might be left [to] the President's discretion. It should be possible [to] provide for situations in which no authorizations f[or] deployment need be sought. But, if a deployme[nt] plainly runs the risk of hostilities, it should have th[e] authorization of Congress.

The President's Conduct of the War

How wide is the presidential power to "co[n]duct" a war? President Nixon's invasion [of] Cambodia in the course of the Vietnam War nice[ly] illustrates the problem. On the assumption th[at] Congress authorized the massive troop commitme[nt] to Vietnam, Professor Bickel concluded that t[he] Cambodian invasion could be sustained under t[he] authority of the Commander-in-Chief, citing t[he] fact that Roosevelt did not seek permission fro[m] Congress to invade North Africa.[133] Witho[ut] pausing to inquire whether the congressional decl[a]ration of war authorized all-out war in eve[ry] possible theater, let it be supposed that Roosev[elt] acted entirely on his own. In that case, we mere[ly] have another presidential "precedent" which ris[es] no higher than the earlier noted "precedents" f[or] unilateral war-making. The perils of unlimit[ed] power to extend the theater of war are exemplifi[ed] by General MacArthur's crossing of the 38th paral[lel] in Korea, which drew powerful Chinese forces in[to] the war.[134] Can it be that an authorization [to] conduct a war against North Korea may [be] stretched into invasion of China on the theory [of] "hot pursuit" or the protection of American troop[s?] Surely the national policy-maker needs to be ask[ed] whether it wants to go so far, to measure the co[st] to the nation against the possible benefits. So mu[ch]

Nixon's invasion of Cambodia to search for a Communist "sanctuary" alone teaches.

No "first General" may create incidents which embroil the nation in war; he may not provoke, extend, or persist in a war against the will of Congress. After conferring upon Congress the lion's share of the war powers, the Framers hardly contemplated that those powers would be suspended or placed in the deep-freeze, once war was commenced. Not only must Congress be consulted before war is begun, it is entitled to be consulted during the war, in Madison's words, whether "a war ought to be commenced, continued or concluded."[135] Shall an expeditionary force be escalated from 60,000 to 500,000 men? That involves vast expenditures, the drafting of many men and replacements, greatly expanded casualties. It is for Congress to decide whether the game is worth the candle. More "confidently" than Professor Henkin, I would, therefore, maintain that the President's

> powers as Commander-in-Chief are subject to ultimate Congressional authority to "make" the war, and Congress can control the conduct of the war it has authorized . . . he would be bound to follow congressional directives not only as to whether to continue the war, but whether to extend it to other countries and other belligerents; whether to fight a limited or unlimited war, today, perhaps, even whether to fight a 'conventional' or a nuclear war.[136]

Enforcement by the Courts

Judicial enforcement of a War Powers Resolution needs to be evaluated in light of the recent decisions directing President Nixon to deliver the White House "tapes" to the Special Prosecutor, and to release impounded funds. This is not to suggest that *United States v. Nixon*[137] established that the courts will enforce a congressional demand for information from the President. That case held that a presidential privilege to withhold "confidential communications" cannot be permitted to impair the administration of justice by the courts; but the rationale of the case extends to an impairment of congressional functions. If the courts may insist on behalf of a criminal defendant upon presidential delivery of information, the Congress stands no

lower in the performance of its even more important functions.[138] In 1965, I urged that there are no jurisdictional barriers — *e.g.* "case or controversy" or "political questions" — to a suit by Congress against the President[139] to enforce a demand for information. Professor Archibald Cox has now added his influential voice: "The Court has often rendered decisions allocating power between the legislative and executive branches, sometimes where there was controversy between them,"[140] as distinguished from controversies between a private person and a federal agency. He concluded that, given an appropriate statute that authorized a district court to entertain an action "by the United States as sovereign to enforce the statutory obligation to provide evidence . . . Congress would be a constitutionally appropriate body to act for the sovereign in the specific enforcement of a law designed solely to assist it in deliberating upon proposed legislation."[141] Recent developments, he continued, "furnish persuasive evidence of a need to increase the power of Congress to compel the President and others in the Executive branch to produce information."[142] These developments "probably make it desirable to put the force of law behind some congressional subpoenas addressed to the President . . ."[143]

Consider next the effect of the impoundment decisions.[144] Though brought by third persons, *e.g.* municipalities and the like, the suits proceeded on the theory that the impoundments were unconstitutional because they invaded the exclusive prerogative of Congress[145] or that they were in violation of statute. It would be highly doctrinaire to maintain that a third person may be heard to complain of the invasion of *congressional* prerogative because he suffers personal loss[146] but that Congress can not be awarded protection against infringement of its own rights. In similar case, Professor Cox stated, "The difference in named parties is probably irrelevant."[147]

The considerations which prompted judicial review in such cases, *e.g.* Truman's seizure of the steel mills in the midst of the Korean war, have far greater weight when a statute expressly limits presidential embarkation on war without prior congressional approval in contravention of the Constitution. The staggering costs of such adventurism are too well known to need recapitulation.

While an obstinate President may defy the Congress —as Nixon defied the Senate Select Committee and the House Judiciary Committee subpoenas in aid of its impeachment inquiry — even the intransigent Nixon turned over the "tapes" to the Special Prosecutor at the command of the Supreme Court. A Court directive to halt all steps towards war would place the influence of the Court behind the statutory requirement, and it is hardly conceivable that a President will resist both Congress and the Court. Such resistance would arouse the nation and another "firestorm"[148] would sweep over the White House.

The prior decisions by the lower courts, dismissing suits to halt the Vietnam War brought by soldiers or individual Congressmen, are distinguishable. The reluctance of courts to permit individuals to decide, in effect, whether or not a war is without constitutional warrant is understandable, the more so as there was evidence of congressional acquiescence in, if not approval of, the war.[149] But a suit by Congress to enforce a statute limiting solo war-making stands quite differently.[150] There, Congress is calling on the President "faithfully to execute the law" which it has enacted, and which is binding on him until it is judicially declared to be unconstitutional.[151] It is asking the Court to protect it from an invasion of its exclusive right to make war, a type of interest courts have often protected.[152] The Court, it seems to me, could ill afford to turn its face from a suit by Congress to prevent a President from plunging the nation into war in defiance of statute.

Impeachment is an unsatisfactory substitute as long as the constitutionality of presidential claims to solo war-making power remains judicially unsettled.[153] Trial by the Congress of its claim that the President has unconstitutionally encroached on its prerogative would represent adjudication by an interested party of his own cause. It is the function of the Court to demark the limits of constitutional power and, if anything, that function is most important when two branches dispute where the boundaries between them lie and the dispute involves the greatest interests of the nation.[154]

A War Powers Act, therefore, should include a provision that would authorize a suit by either House of Congress to direct the President to comply with the statute.

Notes to

PRESIDENTIAL WAR POWERS

by Professor Raoul Berger

1.   Public Law 93-148, 87 Stat.555 (1973).
2.   R. Berger, Executive Privilege: A Constitutional Myth 83 (1974), hereinafter cited as Berger, E.P. Citations thereto rather than the original sources are meant to reduce the mass of citations and to furnish other confirmatory materials.
3.   E. Corwin, The President: Office and Powers 283-306 (3d ed. 1948).
4.   Hearings on War Powers Legislation before Senate Committee on Foreign Relations 261 (92d Cong. 1st Sess. 1971). A. Schlesinger, Jr., The Imperial Presidency 132 (1974).
5.   Sorensen, The Case For a Strong Presidency, in Has the President Too Much Power 24, 26 (C.Roberts ed. 1974). This book will hereinafter be cited as Roberts Ed.
6.   Berger, Constructive Contempt: A Post Mortem, 9 U. Chi. L. Rev. 602, 604-605, 641-642 (1942).
7.   Berger, E.P.91.
8.   Id. at 93.
9.   Griswold v. Connecticut, 381 U.S. 479 522 (1965) dissenting.
10.   Berger, War-Making by the President 121 U. Pa. L. Rev. 29, 32 (1972).
11.   Sorensen, in Roberts ed. supra, n.5 a 29; Bundy, Toward an Open Foreign Policy: The Opportunity and The Problem, in Roberts ed. supra n.5 at 222, 224.
12.   Sundquist stated that Vietnam involve the question "of how the President uses the powe that is assigned to the head of the executiv branch." Sundquist, What Happened to Our Check and Balances, in Roberts ed. supra, n.5 at 96, 9 Cf. Sorensen, id. at 25.
13.   Berger, Impeachment: Some Constit tional Problems 33, 86 (1973).
14.   Berger, supra, n.10 at 30.
15.   Cf. Hargrove, The Power of the Mode Presidency 283 (1974); Senator Howard Bake infra, text accompanying n.102.

16. Part the First, Art. XVIII, 1 B. Poore, Federal and State Constitutions, Colonial Charters 959 (1877).

17. Trial of Horne Tooke, 25 How. St. Tr. 1, 268 (1794).

18. Berger, E.P. 49.

19. Ibid.

20. Ibid.

21. Art. IX; Berger, E.P. 64.

22. Reveley, Constitutional Allocation of the War Powers Between the President and Congress 1787-1788, 15 Va. Jour. Intl. Law 73, 92 (1974).

23. 2 M. Farrand, The Records of the Federal Convention of 1787, p. 182 (1911); Berger, E.P. 65. The effect of the shift from "make" to "declare" is discussed id. at 66-68; Reveley, supra, n.22 at 126-128.

24. Berger, E.P. 61.

25. Ibid.

26. Id. at 62. The Congress instructed him "punctually to observe and follow such orders and directives . . . as you shall receive from this or a future Congress." Ibid.

27. Ibid.

28. See *United States v. Burr*, 25 Fed. Cas. 55, 165 (No. 14693) (C.Ct. Va. 1807).

29. Berger, E.P. 62 n.14; see also id. at 52, 53.

30. Id. at 63; see also Reveley, supra, n.22 at 128-130.

31. Berger, E.P. 63; see also id. at 67 n.39, 68.

32. "Those who are to conduct a war," said Madison, "cannot in the nature of things, be proper or safe judges, whether a war ought to be commenced, continued, or concluded." Id. at 64; see also Rufus King, id. at 67; Hamilton, id. at 67 n. 39; and Roger Sherman, id. at 68. And see Reveley, supra, n.22 at 130, 144.

33. Berger, E.P. 63-64.

34. Id. at 68; emphasis added.

35. Id. at 69.

36. Id. at 67.

37. Reveley, supra, n.22 at 144.

38. Berger, E.P. 70.

39. Rostow, Great Cases Make Bad Law: The War Powers Act, 50 Tex. L. Rev. 833, 847 1972).

40. Professor Alexander Bickel stated about the Framers: "There was no doubt in their minds that the war power was to be legislative. The problem was how to keep the President as effective Commander in Chief. It was not even a shared power, I think, in their minds." Hearings on War Powers before the House Sub-committee on National Security Policy and Scientific Developments 190 (93d Cong. 1st Sess. Mar. 1973), hereinafter cited as Zablocki Hearings.

40a. Berger, E.P. 56.

41. The Federalist, No. 48 at 323 (Mod. Lib. ed. 1937).

42. Berger, E.P. at 54-55.

43. Id. at 57. In Federalist No. 41 at 269, Madison asked, "For what purpose could the enumeration of particular powers be inserted, if these and all others were meant to be included in the preceding general power? Nothing is more natural nor common than first to use a general phrase, and then to explain and qualify it by a recital of particulars."

44. Berger, E.P. at 57-58.

45. 1 M. Farrand, Records of the Federal Convention 1787 at 66-67 (1911), emphasis added. A "definition of their extent," he added, "would assist the judgment in determining how far they might be safely entrusted to a single officer." Ibid.

46. Berger, E.P. 58. John Dickinson also "was of opinion that the powers of the Executive ought to be defined before we say in whom the power shall vest. 1 Farrand, supra, n.45 at 74.

47. 1 Farrand, supra, n.45 at 64-65.

48. Berger, E.P. 52.

49. Bagehot stated that the Constitution-makers feared that the sovereign power "would generate tyranny; George III had been a tyrant to them, and come what might, they would not make a George III." W. Bagehot, The English Constitution 218 (1964). For citations to their deep-seated aversion to monarchy see Berger, E.P. 50 n.8.

50. Berger, E.P. 59. "The weight of the evidence at Philadelphia does suggest that a majority of the Framers by September wished an Executive who would be more than an agent of Congress. But it is difficult to conclude from that intention that the Framers, without saying so, also meant to clothe the President with an indeterminate reservoir of foreign and military authority via the executive power clause, in light of their caution concerning

executive-power and their expressed desire to limit it." Reveley, supra, n. 22 at 123.

51. Federalist No. 48 at 322.

52. Infra, text accompanying n.101.

53. Berger, E.P. 59.

54. The Legality of the United States Participation in Vietnam, 75 Yale L. J. 1085, 1101 (1966).

55. Berger, E.P. 76.

56. F. D. Wormuth, The Vietnam War: The President and the Constitution, in 2 The Vietnam War and International Law 711 (Falk. ed. 1969); Schlesinger, supra, n.4 at 50-64, 89-90; Berger, supra, n.10 at 58-68.

57. Berger, supra, n.10 at 60.

58. Berger, E.P. at 82-83.

59. Berger, supra, n.10 at 60, n.196.

60. Berger, E.P. 75 n.75.

61. Ibid.

62. Id. at 86.

63. Berger, supra, n.10 at 54.

64. *Powell v. McCormack*, 395 U.S. 486, 546-547 (1969): "That an unconstitutional action has been taken before surely does not render that same action any less unconstitutional at a later date." See also *United States v. Morton Salt Co.*, 338 U.S. 632, 647 (1950).

65. Berger, E.P. at 94.

66. Berger, supra, n.10 at 30. Professor Rostow was an executant of the Vietnam policy while a member of the State Department.

67. Zablocki Hearings, supra, n.40 at 502.

68. Id. at 395.

69. Id. at 396. But for some "nuances," we are said to share "congruent positions." Id. at 397. Our views of the "original intention" are now shared by Reveley, supra, n.22.

70. Zablocki Hearings, supra, n.40 at 397, 402.

71. Id. at 397; emphasis added.

72. Id. at 397, 398.

73. Id. at 398. "The Founders considered the power to declare war too important to entrust it to the President alone, or even to him and the Senate, and gave it to the Congress." L. Henkin, Foreign Affairs and the Constitution, 80 (1973).

74. Zablocki Hearings, supra, n.40 at 398.

75. Ibid.

76. Ibid.

77. Id. at 400, 401.

78. Id. at 401.

79. *Youngstown Sheet & Tube Co. v. Sawyer*, 343. U.S. 579, 604 (1952), concurring.

80. R. Berger, *Congress v. The Supreme Court* 235, 369 (1969); *Reid v. Covert*, 354 U.S. 1, 16-17 (1957).

81. Zablocki Hearings, supra, n.40 at 402.

82. Id. at 405. For the common thread of the treaties, see id. at 404.

83. Id. at 405.

84. Id. at 404, 498, 402.

85. Id. at 498.

86. Id. at 498 n.4.

87. Wormuth, supra, n.56 at 776; Note, Congress, the President, and the Power to Commit Forces to Combat in 2 The Vietnam War and International Law 615, 645-646 (Falk. ed. 1969).

88. *Reid v. Covert*, 354 U.S. 1, 16-17 (1957).

89. See Van Alstyne, supra, text accompanying n.73.

90. Zablocki Hearings, supra, n.40 at 400-401.

91. Supra, text accompanying notes 40-53

92. Berger, E.P. 135-137.

93. Id. at 135.

94. Zablocki Hearings, supra, n.40 at 502

95. Berger, E.P. at 135.

96. Id. at 136.

97. Supra, n.79.

98. In his *Letters of Camillus*, Hamilton returned to his earlier view. Berger, E.P. at 137-138

99. Zablocki Hearings, supra, n.40 at 402

100. Rostow, supra, n.39 at 849.

101. Berger, E.P. 95 n.185. For similar remarks by his fellow Justices, see ibid; and see id at 101 n.211.

102. Baker, What Presidential Powers Should Be Cut? in Roberts ed. supra, n.5 at 41.

103. In Federalist No. 69 at 448, Hamilton commented, "The President will have only the occasional command of such part of the militia of the nation as by legislative provision may be called into actual service of the Union."

104. 1 J. Story, Commentaries on the Constitution of the United States §428 (5th ed. 1905).

105. S. 2956, 92d Cong. 2d Sess. §§3, (1972).

106. Schlesinger, Zablocki Hearings, supra, n.40 at 164-165.

107. Id. at 166.

108. Id. at 167.

109. Ibid. "If the nation is divided or united so is Congress likely to be." Hargróve, supra, n.15 at 168.

110. Berger, E.P. 69 n.45.

111. E. Weinband & T. Franck, Resignation in Protest 177 (1975), quoting Bertolt Brecht's "Galileo."

112. Berger, E.P. 345.

113. Supra, n.56.

114. Berger, E.P. 72-73.

115. 17 U.S. (4 Wheat.) 316, 415 (1819).

116. Act of February 28, 1795, ch. 36, §1, 1 Stat. 424. See also Berger, E.P. 73 n.66.

117. 293 U.S. 388, 415 (1935); see also Berger, E.P. 74 n.69.

118. Federalist No. 23 at 142.

119. Berger, E.P. 111.

120 U.S. Constitution, Art. I §8(1).

121. Id. at §8(12).

122. Ibid.; see also Berger, E.P. 112 n.270.

123. Federalist No. 26 at 163; see also Berger, E.P. 112 n.271.

124. Berger, E.P. 113.

125. 12 & 13 Will. 3, c. 11, §26, 3 Statutes at Large 367 (1758).

126. Berger, E.P. 113-114.

127. Public Law No. 91-652, 84 Stat. 1942, 1943.

128. U.S. Constitution, Art. I §8(14).

129. Berger, E.P. 114.

130. Schlesinger reminds us of Elihu Root's statement in the Senate — he had been Secretary of War and Secretary of State — that "Congress could by law forbid the troops' being sent out of the country." Zablocki Hearings, supra, n.40 at 169.

131. Ibid.

132. Id. at 185.

133. Id. at 183.

134. Berger, E.P. 115 n.283.

135. Supra, n.32.

136. Berger, E.P. at 115-116.

137. 94 S.Ct. 3090 (1974).

138. For extended discussion of the effect of that case see Berger, The Incarnation of Executive Privilege, 22 U.C.L.A. L. Rev. 4 (1974).

139. Berger, Executive Privilege v. Congressional Inquiry, 12 U.C.L.A. L. Rev. 1044, 1333-62.

140. Cox, Executive Privilege, 122 U. Pa. L. Rev. 1383, 1422 (1974); Berger, supra, n.158 at 1337-38, 1347-48.

141. Cox, id. at 1424; Berger, id. at 1334-35.

142. Cox, id. at 1432; Berger, id. at 1334.

143. Cox, id. at 1434.

144. The cases are collected in Mikva & Hertz, Impoundment of Funds — The Courts, The Congress and The President: A Constitutional Triangle, 69 N.W. L. Rev. 335, 346 n.53 (1974).

145. For the constitutional issues, see id. at 376-382, 388-389.

146. Compare *Youngstown Sheet & Tube Co. v. Sawyer,* 343 U.S. 579 (1952).

147. Cox, supra, n.162 at 1423; see also Berger, supra, n.161 at 1350-51.

148. The reference is to the indignant protests that flooded the White House after President Nixon discharged Special Prosecutor Archibald Cox.

149. Cf. Berger, E.P. 71 n.53; see also *Orlando v. Laird,* 443 F. 2d 1039, 1042 (2d Cir. 1971). The cases dismissing such suits on "political questions" grounds are collected in *Holtzman v. Schlesinger,* 484 F. 2d 1307, 1312 n.3 (2d Cir. 1973). A vigorous dissent by Justice Douglas from a denial of certiorari in one such case is contained in *Massachusetts v. Laird,* 400 U.S. 886 (1971).

150. Chairman Zablocki, taking note of the suits by individual soldiers stated, "I think the court would think otherwise with a war powers resolution on the books." Zablocki, Can the President's Power be limited in a Nuclear World? in Roberts ed. supra n.5 at 188, 192. Chairman Zablocki misconceives the issue; it is not *"Can* the President's War Powers be limited,"* but, whether they *are* limited by the Constitution.

151. Berger, supra, n.158 at 1114-17.

152. Id. at 1346; see also *Coleman v. Miller,* 307 U.S. 433, 442 (1939).

153. Berger, Impeachment: The Constitutional Problems 291 (1973). Chief Justice Chase suggested that the issue in the Andrew Johnson impeachment should have been submitted to the courts. Id. at 295.

154. R. Berger, id. at 291; L. Hand, The Bill of Rights 3, 15 (1962).

APPENDIX: WAR POWERS RESOLUTION

Public Law 93-148
93rd Congress, H. J. Res. 542
November 7, 1973

𝕵𝖔𝖎𝖓𝖙 𝕽𝖊𝖘𝖔𝖑𝖚𝖙𝖎𝖔𝖓

Concerning the war powers of Congress and the President.

*Resolved by the Senate and House of Representatives of the United
States of America in Congress assembled,*

War Powers
Resolution.

SHORT TITLE

SECTION 1. This joint resolution may be cited as the "War Powers
Resolution".

PURPOSE AND POLICY

SEC. 2. (a) It is the purpose of this joint resolution to fulfill the
intent of the framers of the Constitution of the United States and
insure that the collective judgment of both the Congress and the
President will apply to the introduction of United States Armed
Forces into hostilities, or into situations where imminent involvement
in hostilities is clearly indicated by the circumstances, and to the continued use of such forces in hostilities or in such situations.

(b) Under article I, section 8, of the Constitution, it is specifically
provided that the Congress shall have the power to make all laws necessary and proper for carrying into execution, not only its own powers
but also all other powers vested by the Constitution in the Government of the United States, or in any department or officer thereof.

USC prec.
title 1.

(c) The constitutional powers of the President as Commander-in-
Chief to introduce United States Armed Forces into hostilities, or
into situations where imminent involvement in hostilities is clearly
indicated by the circumstances, are exercised only pursuant to (1) a
declaration of war, (2) specific statutory authorization, or (3) a
national emergency created by attack upon the United States, its territories or possessions, or its armed forces.

CONSULTATION

SEC. 3. The President in every possible instance shall consult with
Congress before introducing United States Armed Forces into hostilities or into situations where imminent involvement in hostilities is
clearly indicated by the circumstances, and after every such introduction shall consult regularly with the Congress until United States
Armed Forces are no longer engaged in hostilities or have been removed
from such situations.

REPORTING

SEC. 4. (a) In the absence of a declaration of war, in any case in
which United States Armed Forces are introduced—

(1) into hostilities or into situations where imminent involvement in hostilities is clearly indicated by the circumstances;

87 STAT. 555

(2) into the territory, airspace or waters of a foreign nation,
while equipped for combat, except for deployments which relate
solely to supply, replacement, repair, or training of such forces;
or

87 STAT. 556

(3) in numbers which substantially enlarge United States
Armed Forces equipped for combat already located in a foreign
nation;

58

the President shall submit within 48 hours to the Speaker of the House of Representatives and to the President pro tempore of the Senate a report, in writing, setting forth—

    (A) the circumstances necessitating the introduction of United States Armed Forces;

    (B) the constitutional and legislative authority under which such introduction took place; and

    (C) the estimated scope and duration of the hostilities or involvement.

(b) The President shall provide such other information as the Congress may request in the fulfillment of its constitutional responsibilities with respect to committing the Nation to war and to the use of United States Armed Forces abroad.

(c) Whenever United States Armed Forces are introduced into hostilities or into any situation described in subsection (a) of this section, the President shall, so long as such armed forces continue to be engaged in such hostilities or situation, report to the Congress periodically on the status of such hostilities or situation as well as on the scope and duration of such hostilities or situation, but in no event shall he report to the Congress less often than once every six months.

CONGRESSIONAL ACTION

SEC. 5. (a) Each report submitted pursuant to section 4(a)(1) shall be transmitted to the Speaker of the House of Representatives and to the President pro tempore of the Senate on the same calendar day. Each report so transmitted shall be referred to the Committee on Foreign Affairs of the House of Representatives and to the Committee on Foreign Relations of the Senate for appropriate action. If, when the report is transmitted, the Congress has adjourned sine die or has adjourned for any period in excess of three calendar days, the Speaker of the House of Representatives and the President pro tempore of the Senate, if they deem it advisable (or if petitioned by at least 30 percent of the membership of their respective Houses) shall jointly request the President to convene Congress in order that it may consider the report and take appropriate action pursuant to this section.

(b) Within sixty calendar days after a report is submitted or is required to be submitted pursuant to section 4(a)(1), whichever is earlier, the President shall terminate any use of United States Armed Forces with respect to which such report was submitted (or required to be submitted), unless the Congress (1) has declared war or has enacted a specific authorization for such use of United States Armed Forces, (2) has extended by law such sixty-day period, or (3) is physically unable to meet as a result of an armed attack upon the United States. Such sixty-day period shall be extended for not more than an additional thirty days if the President determines and certifies to the Congress in writing that unavoidable military necessity respecting the safety of United States Armed Forces requires the continued use of such armed forces in the course of bringing about a prompt removal of such forces.

(c) Notwithstanding subsection (b), at any time that United States Armed Forces are engaged in hostilities outside the territory of the United States, its possessions and territories without a declaration of war or specific statutory authorization, such forces shall be removed by the President if the Congress so directs by concurrent resolution.

87 STAT. 556
87 STAT. 557

CONGRESSIONAL PRIORITY PROCEDURES FOR JOINT RESOLUTION OR BILL

SEC. 6. (a) Any joint resolution or bill introduced pursuant to section 5(b) at least thirty calendar days before the expiration of the sixty-day period specified in such section shall be referred to the Committee on Foreign Affairs of the House of Representatives or the Committee on Foreign Relations of the Senate, as the case may be, and such committee shall report one such joint resolution or bill, together with its recommendations, not later than twenty-four calendar days before the expiration of the sixty-day period specified in such section, unless such House shall otherwise determine by the yeas and nays.

(b) Any joint resolution or bill so reported shall become the pending business of the House in question (in the case of the Senate the time for debate shall be equally divided between the proponents and the opponents), and shall be voted on within three calendar days thereafter, unless such House shall otherwise determine by yeas and nays.

(c) Such a joint resolution or bill passed by one House shall be referred to the committee of the other House named in subsection (a) and shall be reported out not later than fourteen calendar days before the expiration of the sixty-day period specified in section 5(b). The joint resolution or bill so reported shall become the pending business of the House in question and shall be voted on within three calendar days after it has been reported, unless such House shall otherwise determine by yeas and nays.

(d) In the case of any disagreement between the two Houses of Congress with respect to a joint resolution or bill passed by both Houses, conferees shall be promptly appointed and the committee of conference shall make and file a report with respect to such resolution or bill not later than four calendar days before the expiration of the sixty-day period specified in section 5(b). In the event the conferees are unable to agree within 48 hours, they shall report back to their respective Houses in disagreement. Notwithstanding any rule in either House concerning the printing of conference reports in the Record or concerning any delay in the consideration of such reports, such report shall be acted on by both Houses not later than the expiration of such sixty-day period.

CONGRESSIONAL PRIORITY PROCEDURES FOR CONCURRENT RESOLUTION

SEC. 7. (a) Any concurrent resolution introduced pursuant to section 5(c) shall be referred to the Committee on Foreign Affairs of the House of Representatives or the Committee on Foreign Relations of the Senate, as the case may be, and one such concurrent resolution shall be reported out by such committee together with its recommendations within fifteen calendar days, unless such House shall otherwise determine by the yeas and nays.

(b) Any concurrent resolution so reported shall become the pending business of the House in question (in the case of the Senate the time for debate shall be equally divided between the proponents and the opponents) and shall be voted on within three calendar days thereafter, unless such House shall otherwise determine by yeas and nays.

(c) Such a concurrent resolution passed by one House shall be referred to the committee of the other House named in subsection (a) and shall be reported out by such committee together with its recommendations within fifteen calendar days and shall thereupon become the pending business of such House and shall be voted upon within

87 STAT. 558

three calendar days, unless such House shall otherwise determine by yeas and nays.

(d) In the case of any disagreement between the two Houses of Congress with respect to a concurrent resolution passed by both Houses, conferees shall be promptly appointed and the committee of conference shall make and file a report with respect to such concurrent resolution within six calendar days after the legislation is referred to the committee of conference. Notwithstanding any rule in either House concerning the printing of conference reports in the Record or concerning any delay in the consideration of such reports, such report shall be acted on by both Houses not later than six calendar days after the conference report is filed. In the event the conferees are unable to agree within 48 hours, they shall report back to their respective Houses in disagreement.

INTERPRETATION OF JOINT RESOLUTION

SEC. 8. (a) Authority to introduce United States Armed Forces into hostilities or into situations wherein involvement in hostilities is clearly indicated by the circumstances shall not be inferred—

(1) from any provision of law (whether or not in effect before the date of the enactment of this joint resolution), including any provision contained in any appropriation Act, unless such provision specifically authorizes the introduction of United States Armed Forces into hostilities or into such situations and states that it is intended to constitute specific statutory authorization within the meaning of this joint resolution; or

(2) from any treaty heretofore or hereafter ratified unless such treaty is implemented by legislation specifically authorizing the introduction of United States Armed Forces into hostilities or into such situations and stating that it is intended to constitute specific statutory authorization within the meaning of this joint resolution.

(b) Nothing in this joint resolution shall be construed to require any further specific statutory authorization to permit members of United States Armed Forces to participate jointly with members of the armed forces of one or more foreign countries in the headquarters operations of high-level military commands which were established prior to the date of enactment of this joint resolution and pursuant to the United Nations Charter or any treaty ratified by the United States prior to such date.

59 Stat. 1031.

"Introduction of United States Armed Forces."

(c) For purposes of this joint resolution, the term "introduction of United States Armed Forces" includes the assignment of members of such armed forces to command, coordinate, participate in the movement of, or accompany the regular or irregular military forces of any foreign country or government when such military forces are engaged, or there exists an imminent threat that such forces will become engaged, in hostilities.

(d) Nothing in this joint resolution—

(1) is intended to alter the constitutional authority of the Congress or of the President, or the provisions of existing treaties; or

(2) shall be construed as granting any authority to the President with respect to the introduction of United States Armed Forces into hostilities or into situations wherein involvement in hostilities is clearly indicated by the circumstances which authority he would not have had in the absence of this joint resolution.

SEPARABILITY CLAUSE

SEC. 9. If any provision of this joint resolution or the application thereof to any person or circumstance is held invalid, the remainder of the joint resolution and the application of such provision to any other person or circumstance shall not be affected thereby.

EFFECTIVE DATE

SEC. 10. This joint resolution shall take effect on the date of its enactment.

CARL ALBERT

Speaker of the House of Representatives.

JAMES O. EASTLAND

President of the Senate pro tempore.

IN THE HOUSE OF REPRESENTATIVES, U.S., *November 7, 1973.*

The House of Representatives having proceeded to reconsider the resolution (H. J. Res. 542) entitled "Joint resolution concerning the war powers of Congress and the President", returned by the President of the United States with his objections, to the House of Representatives, in which it originated, it was

Resolved, That the said resolution pass, two-thirds of the House of Representatives agreeing to pass the same.

Attest:

W. PAT JENNINGS *Clerk.*

I certify that this Joint Resolution originated in the House of Representatives.

W. PAT JENNINGS *Clerk.*

IN THE SENATE OF THE UNITED STATES   *November 7, 1973.*

The Senate having proceeded to reconsider the joint resolution (H. J. Res. 542) entitled "Joint resolution concerning the war powers of Congress and the President", returned by the President of the United States with his objections to the House of Representatives, in which it originated, it was

87 STAT. 559
87 STAT. 560

Resolved, That the said joint resolution pass, two-thirds of the Senators present having voted in the affirmative.

Attest:

FRANCIS R. VALEO *Secretary.*

LEGISLATIVE HISTORY:

HOUSE REPORTS: No. 93-287 (Comm. on Foreign Affairs) and No. 93-547
          (Comm. of Conference).
SENATE REPORT No. 93-220 accompanying S. 440 (Comm. on Foreign
          Relations).
CONGRESSIONAL RECORD, Vol. 119 (1973):
     June 25, July 18, considered and passed House.
     July 18 - 20, considered and passed Senate, amended, in
          lieu of S. 440.
     Oct. 10, Senate agreed to conference report.
     Oct. 12, House agreed to conference report.
WEEKLY COMPILATION OF PRESIDENTIAL DOCUMENTS, Vol. 9, No. 43:
     Oct. 24, vetoed; Presidential message.
CONGRESSIONAL RECORD, Vol. 119 (1973):
     Nov. 7, House and Senate overrode veto.

PRESIDENTIAL POWER IN FOREIGN AFFAIRS *

by Professor Louis Henkin
Hamilton Fish Professor of International Law and Diplomacy
and Professor of Constitutional Law
Columbia University School of Law

Again, as periodically in the two centuries of our national life, our unique form of government is the subject of sharp debate. In the wake of Watergate and Vietnam, the focus is on the Presidency, and there are proposals for change, all of them designed to define and contain Executive Power. Vietnam has reopened even issues of Presidential power in foreign affairs, where Presidents have long enjoyed predominance, some think virtual monopoly.

To discuss Presidential power is, of course, to discuss all the divisions and separations of our constitutional system, in particular the distribution of authority between President and Congress. To focus on Presidential power in foreign affairs requires that we pretend that foreign affairs are self-defining, that the President's foreign affairs powers are separable from other Presidential power, that relations between President and Congress in regard to foreign affairs can be isolated from their relations generally.**

I. THE CONSTITUTIONAL BLUEPRINT

I begin with the Constitution. The foreign relations of the United States cannot be understood in the light of the Constitution alone, but they cannot be understood without it, for it continues to shape the institutions and the actions that determine them. Even the extra-constitutional instrumentalities and processes which often seem to dominate the conduct of foreign relations are offspring of the Constitution and of needs created by its blueprint for government. If the Constitution says nothing about the Secretaries of State, Defense,

Treasury; of the National Security Council or the CIA; of the President as leader, as "representative of all the people," as chief of his party, as hero or scapegoat; if it says nothing about Congressional committees, seniority or Senatorial courtesy; all of these can be traced to the Constitution, some to its special treatment of foreign affairs. The impassioned debate scattering blame for our misfortunes in Indochina swirled about the Constitution, implying that the constitutional blueprint for conducting our foreign relations was somehow at fault, and the suggested remedies have included various constitutional amendments. We will have to look far beyond the corners of that document and the conceptions of our Fathers of 1787, but surely we must begin there.

I begin with an "overview" of the constitutional "system" as conceived, and as we now have it. The provisions in the Constitution which explicitly allocate authority and responsibility in foreign affairs are few. Essentially, Congress is given power to regulate commerce with foreign nations, and to decide for war or peace. (The power of Congress to define piracy and offenses against the law of nations has not loomed large in our national history.) The President has the power to make treaties, and to appoint ambassadors, both subject to the consent of the Senate. He also receives ambassadors.

There are also enumerated powers of general applicability which have important uses for foreign affairs. Congress has the power to tax and spend for the common defense and for the general welfare. It can raise and support an army and a navy. It can establish and regulate executive offices. It can legislate, and can appropriate funds, as is necessary

*With some changes, this paper derives from " 'A More Effective System' For Foreign Relations: The Constitutional Framework," a statement I made in May 1974 to the Commission on the Organization of the Government for the Conduct of Foreign Policy. That paper and others are published in Appendix L, Volume V, Report of the Commission, June 1975 and in the May 1975 issue of the Virginia Law Review. There as here I have also drawn on my book *Foreign Affairs and the Constitution* (Foundation Press, 1972). Permissions to use statement and book are gratefully acknowledged.

*Since Raoul Berger is writing separately on the President as Commander-in-Chief, I must pretend also to separate and largely leave to him Presidential powers to deploy armed forces for foreign policy purposes.

and proper to carry out its various powers and those of the other branches of government. For the President, authority to appoint officers (with the advice and consent of the Senate, or alone upon authorization from Congress), his responsibility to see that the laws are faithfully executed, and his command of the armed forces, are as relevant for foreign as for domestic affairs.

Obviously, the enumerated powers were important to the Founding Fathers; they are important today and, contrary to common impression, as constitutional powers, they remain essentially unchanged, and raise few legal issues. The uncertainties and the sources of controversy about the constitutional blueprint lie in what the Constitution does not say. For the enumerated powers relating to foreign affairs, even as supplemented by the powers of general applicability, are spare, leaving much unsaid. For obvious examples, the power to make treaties is allocated to the President-and-Senate, but who has authority to terminate treaties? Congress has the power to declare war, but who can make peace? More importantly, who formulates the foreign policy which is neither a regulation of commerce nor a declaration of war, and which is not embodied in a treaty? Indeed, who formulates general principles of national policy of which commerce and war-or-peace and treaties are particular expressions? And who controls, supervises, and regulates the conduct of our relations with other nations?

These lacunae have moved some of us to speculate whether our Founding Fathers had a limited conception of foreign affairs; or, even, whether they had a conception of the Constitution different from ours — selective rather than complete, immediate rather than eternal, a suggestive guide for reasonable men in their time rather than a tight legal document to be parsed and argued about by lawyers and judges for centuries. Whatever the reason for Constitutional inarticulation, no one has doubted that the United States has the missing powers cited and all other powers possessed by other sovereign nations, and that these powers are in the federal government; what has been uncertain is, which branch of that government has the constitutional authority to act for the United States.

There is a basis for arguing that, for the Constitutional Fathers, the President was to have been the agent and executor of Congressional policy in foreign as in domestic affairs. Some have suggested — with a nod to the Supreme Court's opinion in the Steel Seizure Case — that the inarticulated foreign relations powers of the United States should be divided "naturally," those inherently "executive" allocated to the President, those "legislative" in character to Congress. But is formulating national foreign policy, other than that contained or reflected in statutes, "legislative?" To the contrary, Alexander Hamilton early launched the argument that when the Constitution vested in the President "the Executive Power" (not only, as for Congress, the powers "herein granted"), it included much more than the responsibility of executing Congressional policy; it gave him also a different, independent authority known to the Framers (by way of Montesquieu and Locke) as "executive power," *i.e.*, full powers in foreign relations — except, of course, as the Constitution expressly provided otherwise. That view has not been authoritatively accepted by the courts; but neither has it been rejected. For the rest, lawyers have sought to locate the "missing" pieces of our "system" by construing and interpreting, by interpolating in and extrapolating from what is expressly provided; but they have not achieved any notable consensus.

Constitutional exegesis has not been irrelevant, but especially since argument and authority are available for two (or more) possible principles of distribution of authority, interpretation has not determined the shape of the constitutional "system" — not, in particular, the respective authority of the President and of Congress. They have been shaped primarily by the character and the needs of foreign relations, responding to the respective constitutional and political power of Presidents and Congresses in our system generally, and by the influence of particular Presidents and Congresses at particular times in our history.

Both Congress and the President have assumed powers not specified in the Constitution. In addition to its enumerated powers and their implications, Congress has achieved an unenumerated power to make laws in matters implied in "sovereignty" and "nationhood," *e.g.*, immigration, regulation of nationality, the conduct of nationals abroad, and other matters relating to the conduct of foreign relations — *e.g.*, protecting diplomats. But domestic gislation apart, power to act where the Constitution was silent began to flow to the President from the beginning. For Hamilton that was the result the Constitution intended; intended or not, it was perhaps the inevitable consequence of other constitutional dispositions.

The reasons why the President early acquired dominant influence in foreign policy are relevant to understanding our present system and to any recommendations for improving it. From the beginning the President represented the United States to the world. He was the sole organ of communication with other governments and had exclusive control of the channels and of the processes of communication, usually discrete, often secret. The President had charge of daily relations with other nations. Continuous intercourse generated innumerable issues, and someone had to formulate United States policy about them.

The President began to make that policy. Small decisions in daily intercourse inevitably were made "on the spot," by those engaged in the process. The President also decided many discrete, larger issues. He was always in session and Congress was not, and could not be convened — especially in our early days — without serious difficulty. The President could act alone when Congress was not in session and decision was urgent. He had the facts, and the advice of expert subordinates. He could act quickly and decisively. George Washington — scrupulous, responsible, non-self-aggrandizing — proclaimed neutrality, sent the misbehaving French Minister home, fought Indians, launched the Jay Treaty. He, and his cabinet, and his ambassadors, made a myriad of smaller decisions — formulated national policy — in conducting relations with other countries every day.

The President's control of the conduct of foreign relations, I stress, has brought with it large powers to formulate foreign policy. The President formulates policy when he makes claims on behalf of the United States, or responds to claims or other overtures by foreign governments. The conduct of foreign relations itself inevitably communicates attitudes and intentions; it entails, or leads to, understandings, commitments, agreements. From the Monroe Doctrine and earlier, to the Nixon Doctrine and since, Presidents developed and announced prospective national policy committing the United States to directions and future action, and other states treated these declarations as United States policy. (Compare the accusations in April 1975 that the United States had defaulted on its commitments to the leaders of South Vietnam.) An Executive Branch responsible for foreign relations could not avoid planning and projecting national attitudes and policies; if some of these might eventually call for a treaty, a statute, a declaration of war, or an appropriation of funds, Congress will become necessary, but it need not be involved before it becomes necessary.

From the beginning Presidents began to make even formal executive agreements, written as well as oral, many not unimportant. The Senate could not complain about those it did not know of; it did not complain of many it knew of; occasional complaints did not challenge or affect the President's asserted power in principle.

As the President established sole control of the conduct of foreign relations and achieved the authority to formulate national foreign policy, other Presidential functions also assumed policy-making character. The power to appoint ambassadors (with the consent of the Senate) and the task of receiving foreign ambassadors, became authority to recognize (or not recognize) states and governments, and to begin, terminate, or resume relations with them. The power to appoint other officers (with the consent of the Senate, or alone, by legislative authorization), and the early practice of appointing special agents for *ad hoc* assignments without Senate consent, were used to further presidential policies. The President's tasks of seeing that the laws are faithfully executed, and of defending United States interests around the world, became authority to use the armed forces under his command — short of war — for these purposes, and generally for implementing treaties, laws, and national policies (including Presidential foreign policy).

Congress contributed to the early and continuing growth of Presidential power in foreign affairs (though, perhaps, it could not have prevented it). Congress early recognized and confirmed the President's control of daily foreign intercourse. It did not organize itself, or equip itself with expertise, so that it might pretend to dominate authority in foreign relations, or even a continuous, informed

Iraq came out of faithful execution + protection of Amer. interests + Vietnam, Bush knows his job! → inst. anger

65

participation in them. It did not, and was not equipped to, consider, plan, and resolve foreign policy generally, and any constitutional power which it may have had to do so soon atrophied. It did not, and was not equipped to, follow closely what the President was doing and it did not often bestir itself to disown or to dissociate itself from what the President had done, to condemn him for doing it, or even to question his authority to do it. When issues of authority arose, they became enmeshed in partisan dispute, the President's party in Congress generally defending his authority, the opposition's strictures becoming, or appearing, partisan rather than principled, institutional, constitutional.

Congressmen sometimes grumbled or even "reserved their positions," but usually acquiesced; rarely did Congress resist formally. Often, informal consultations with Congressional leaders disarmed Congressmen who might have been disposed to constitutional battle, and thus helped confirm Presidential authority to act without formal Congressional participation. Congress conceded and compounded Presidential primacy when it began, early, to delegate to him huge grants of power with only general lines to guide him, thus effectively leaving to him the formulation of policy, as well as large discretion in carrying it out.

In a word, Congress allowed itself to become removed from the *process* of conducting foreign relations and formulating foreign policy, appearing in it only late when formal Congressional (or Senate) action was constitutionally required, and in an independent, almost adversary posture vis-à-vis the Executive. By then, Congress often did not feel free to refuse to consummate policies which the President had developed for the United States, thus effectively confirming his authority to make them.

In time, the issue became not whether the President had authority to act but what were the limits on his authority; not whether the President could act when Congress was silent, but, even, whether he could act contrary to the expressed wishes of Congress; whether Congress could direct, control or supersede his decisions; whether Congress was constitutionally free *not* to implement his policies by appropriations or legislation.

I have emphasized Presidential power to formulate foreign policy and its roots in his control of foreign relations. That emphasis, however, does not depreciate the part which Congress continues to have in the formulation of foreign policy. Congress formulates major foreign policy by legislation regulating commerce with foreign nations or authorizing international trade agreements. The Foreign Commerce Power has grown enormously on the wings of the Interstate Commerce Power so that Congress now has nearly-unlimited power to regulate anything that is, is in, or affects, either interstate or foreign commerce. Congress also — and Congress alone — has the power to formulate national policy to go to war or to stay at peace; Congress has also determined United States neutrality in the wars of others. The War Powers of Congress include the power to legislate and spend as necessary to wage war successfully; to prepare for war, or to deter or defend against war; to deal with the consequences of war. Under the "general welfare" clause, Congress can decide where, for what, how much, and on what conditions to spend — as in foreign aid. There are implications for foreign policy when Congress establishes and regulates the Foreign Service and the bureaucracy of various departments and agencies dealing with foreign affairs. The innumerable uses of the "necessary and proper" clause include many that "formulate foreign policy." Since foreign policy and foreign relations require money, which only Congress can appropriate, Congress has some voice in all foreign policy through the appropriations process (although Congress would probably not be constitutionally justified in refusing to finance policies which are within the President's power to make). Congress's unenumerated power to legislate on all matters relating to "nationhood" and foreign affairs may reach far beyond regulation of immigration, nationality and diplomacy; and it includes, apparently, the power to join the President in making international agreements by resolution of both houses of Congress, as an alternative to the treaty process.

The Senate, in its executive capacity, is indispensable to the formulation of foreign policy by treaty — as, in our day, in the United Nations (UN) Charter, the North Atlantic Treaty, or even common treaties of Friendship, Commerce and Navigation. If the Senate does not often formally refuse consent to treaties, it sometimes achieves that result simply by failing to act on them. Sometimes it gives consent only with important reservations. When the Senate consents to an important treaty, it is often because its views were anticipated or informally determined and taken into account. Occasionally the Senate contributes to national policy and its formulation by its actions and expressed attitudes on appointments of foreign service officers, cabinet members and other important officials in the "foreign affairs establishment."

I have been describing the formulation of foreign policy; its implementation is, in constitutional terms, more easily described. The President (through the State Department, the Foreign Service, other departments and agencies), implements all foreign policy, that made by the President, the President-and-Senate, or the Congress. Congress implements foreign policy by enacting necessary and proper legislation and by appropriating funds.

Summary

For convenience and clarity I sum up the system I have described.

American foreign policy is made explicitly by statute or resolution, by international agreement, by unilateral executive acts and declarations; foreign policy is implied in appointments, in the means and the manner by which policy is implemented and foreign relations are conducted. Foreign policy is implemented by statute and appropriation of funds, by Presidential order and action, by a myriad of actions of a host of officials, within the United States and abroad, in the conduct of relations every day. In summary form:

Formulation of Policy

a. Congress formulates foreign policy by legislation or resolution:

— regulating international trade and commerce, or delegating authority to the President to promulgate regulations or to negotiate international agreements to that end;

— declaring war or peace or neutrality, raising armies and otherwise preparing for war or defending against the possibility of war, mobilizing the country for successful war, or dealing with the consequences of war;

— defining offenses against the law of nations and exercising powers inherent in sovereignty and nationhood and other powers related to foreign affairs;

— enacting law or appropriating funds necessary and proper to carry out Congressional policies, international agreements, or other Presidential policies;

— taxing and spending for the common defense and the general welfare.

Congress also contributes to policy by investigation, in aid of appropriations or legislation, and by other formal and informal acts of committees and individuals.

b. The Senate in its executive capacity contributes to foreign policy by granting or denying consent to Presidential treaties and appointments, by imposing reservations or conditions on its consent to treaties, and by communicating views and attitudes in the course of its deliberations.

c. The President formulates foreign policy by:

— making treaties, with the consent of the Senate, and executive agreements pursuant to treaty, Congressional delegation (or subject to its approval) or on his own authority;

— appointing Ambassadors, foreign service and civil service officers (with the consent of the Senate, or alone pursuant to Congressional legislation) or special agents for foreign missions;

— recognizing or not recognizing foreign states or governments (or foreign conquest or the status of belligerency or insurgency), and by maintaining or interrupting relations with foreign governments;

— making and settling international claims on behalf of the U.S. and responding to claims and other overtures by other states;

— formally declaring "doctrines" and other policy;

— making informal commitments, undertakings and understandings, and reflecting general attitudes in the daily conduct of foreign relations.

Foreign policy is implied also in the means and methods chosen to implement it, notably in decisions of whether to use force to that end.

Implementation

Different policies require implementation in different forms and by different processes. In general, foreign policy is implemented by the

President and the Executive Establishment, whether by particular acts or in the conduct of foreign relations generally; some policy is implemented by *ad hoc* agencies created by Congress. Congress implements foreign policy by legislation and appropriation of funds.

I have described the constitutional system for formulating foreign policy. "Sub-constitutionally," all know, "the President" is a huge bureaucracy in the Department of State and in other departments and agencies, and in more than a hundred missions throughout the world. Congress, too, is much beside the formal statutes and resolutions it adopts, and, formally and informally, Congressional committees and individual Congressmen contribute to policy in many ways and instances. For my purposes, the sub-constitutional institutions and procedures depend on and derive from the formal constitutional parts of President, Congress and Senate, and are only the machinery whereby the constitutional roles are played. Of course, the effectiveness of the constitutional system may depend on the organization and operation within each branch and on relations between branches, as much as — perhaps more than — on the underlying constitutional blueprint. Improvement in this "subsystem," moreover, is surely easier and might be more effective than surgery on the basic structure by constitutional amendment.

II. UNCERTAINTIES AND INADEQUACIES

Some are of the view that the system we now have does not conform to the "original understanding," or even to the principles of the Constitution as it has developed; that there has been usurpation (notably by the President) or abdication (by Congress), or both, which should be rectified. Others, eschewing notions of constitutional distortion or impropriety, believe that the system we have has not worked as intended, or, in any event, has not worked well, and they seek changes to make it work better. While most objections challenge Presidential actions, Presidents have sometimes claimed that Congress has acted improperly and there have been suggestions for improving Congressional behavior as well.

Issues of Congressional Power

There are few issues as to the powers of Congress to formulate or implement foreign policy. Presidents do not deny Congressional authority to legislate trade policy and domestic law relevant to foreign affairs; to decide for war or peace (including neutrality if that concept and status still exist in contemporary international law); to spend, to appropriate, to investigate. Congress has not been asserting power to declare foreign policy by resolution, to denounce treaties, to recognize or deny recognition to governments, to control international negotiations or the daily conduct of foreign relations.

Essentially the live issues as to Congressional power are of two kinds. Presidents have denied the authority of Congress to exercise its powers in ways that conflict with Presidential powers or policies. Congress, it has been argued, cannot tell the President — as it seems to have done in the War Powers Resolution — where to deploy or not to deploy forces, or regulate his authority to use them, in circumstances short of war; or govern his discretion as commander-in-chief during war, as in regard to bombing in Cambodia in 1973. Presidents have objected to directions to spend, and to limitations and conditions on spending, that go counter to Presidential policies. For example, President Truman resisted a directive to lend money to Franco Spain; other Presidents objected to clauses barring foreign aid to named countries or those committed to some ideology or policy, or imposing conditions on voluntary contributions to the UN. In foreign affairs, as elsewhere, Presidents have also claimed Congressional "usurpation" when it seeks to use concurrent resolutions and other forms of "legislative veto" (rather than formal legislation which would be subject to Presidential veto) to terminate authority delegated to the President or to scrutinize and regulate his execution of that authority.

Presidents have also asserted, and Congressmen have denied, the obligation of Congress to adopt legislation and appropriate funds to implement treaties and other Presidential policy. In fact however, Congress has not failed to implement or appropriate. (There might, of course, be differences between President and Congress as to the implementation called for, especially as to amounts of money required; and Congress might refuse to implement where it denied the President's authority to formulate the particular policy.)

Issues of Presidential Power

In recent years, all know, there has been sharp debate about Presidential authority to use the armed forces of the United States in hostilities without declaration of war or other authorization by Congress. In large part, these debates have centered on the meaning and purpose of resolutions (*e.g.*, Tonkin Gulf), reflecting on Presidential credibility and integrity and Congressional gullibility, on the effectiveness of our system; but some differences on constitutional principle also emerged. Presidents have insisted, in effect, that they have constitutional authority to deploy the armed forces to implement foreign policy, short of sending them to war. Congressmen — and Congress, in the War Powers Resolution — have denied the President's independent authority to deploy the troops where they would or are likely to be engaged "in hostilities," apparently even "short of war," except in emergency created by attack on U.S. territory or on our armed forces.

A major issue of principle has been the scope of the President's power to conclude executive agreements on his authority. No President has claimed authority to dispense with Senate consent in all cases; few Senators would deny the President the power to make any "sole" agreements whatsoever. No one, however, has offered a generally acceptable line distinguishing agreements which the President can make on his own authority from those which constitutionally require Senate consent. Even "importance" is not the touchstone, whether in principle or in practice: the "sole" executive agreement has been accepted for important agreements which, from diplomatic necessity or other national interest, should be kept confidential. (A different, small unresolved issue is the domestic legal effect of an executive agreement, especially in the face of an earlier inconsistent statute.)

The other issues and uncertainties of Presidential power in foreign affairs are instances of such difficulties in Presidential-Congressional relations generally. In foreign affairs, executive privilege and the need for secrecy (even from Congress) are asserted more often and more plausibly. All agree that there is need for some secrecy, and that the Executive Branch is entitled to some "privacy." See

United States v. Nixon, 418 U.S. 685 (1974). The question is how much and in what circumstances, and how and by whom these shall be determined. Can Congress prevent "unnecessary" secrecy, and non-disclosure which it deems to be not bona fide?

Impoundment, too, is not particularly a foreign-affairs issue, though the temptation, and perhaps the justification, for impounding may be greater when Congress insists on spending or appropriating for purposes which are inconsistent with Presidential foreign policy. Congress has now legislated to regulate impoundment, and the Supreme Court has recently rejected impoundment in a domestic case, though it did not explicitly address the President's constitutional claims. Compare *Train v. City of New York,* 420 U.S. 35 (1975). In general, I have not been able to find any constitutional basis for the President's alleged power: the responsibility to see to it that the laws are faithfully executed would not seem to imply authority not to execute them. But there is stronger — I do not say strong — argument that the President may impound, against the wishes of Congress, monies appropriated for foreign affairs purposes of which the President disapproves.

Systemic "Ineffectiveness"

Diagnosis of deficiencies in the system I have described, and the quest for a more effective system, must face the implications of the separation of powers. For our Constitutional Fathers, surely, "effectiveness" was not the sole or the principal desideratum. As Mr. Justice Brandeis reminded us, they made separation of powers the animating principle of the Constitution "not to promote efficiency"; the "inevitable friction" resulting from separation, he said, was purposeful, "to preclude the exercise of arbitrary power." *Myers v. United States,* 272 U.S. 52, 293 (1926) (dissenting opinion).

Our system for formulating and implementing foreign policy, then, is inherently and purposefully less "effective" than it might be if foreign policy were made and implemented under a single constitutional authority, say, the President. To some, surely, the need for Senate consent to the treaty or to a Presidential appointment makes our system less "effective." To some — including John Quincy Adams — lodging the power to declare war in

Congress was an "absurdity." The "ineffectiveness" produced by such separation is in substantial measure responsible for modifications or circumventions — for the growth and acceptance of Presidential agents, Presidential agreements, Presidential "wars" or hostilities-short-of-war.

The principal "ineffectiveness" of our system, I believe, is that the separation of powers and responsibilities in foreign affairs has not worked as originally intended, and in some respects has not worked well. Where originally, I believe, the principal authority in foreign policy was probably intended for Congress, the character of international affairs, and the growing importance of daily routine relations, have given the President the dominant part, not subject to effective check or balance. In the result, the formulation of foreign policy is essentially bifurcated, with Congress retaining the constitutional authority which had been expressly given it (commerce, spending, war-and-peace), and the President formulating other foreign policy. But foreign policy is "seamless" and interdependent and having different parts of it formulated by different, separate branches is inevitably "ineffective." Some may find the particular division which separates trade and spending and war from other policy particularly ineffective.

Even more, *the President's control of international communication and of the daily conduct of foreign relations has made it difficult — perhaps impossible — for Congress to exercise its constitutional powers and responsibilities effectively, "separately."* Even in domestic affairs the President has become a principal source, initiator, planner, draftsman of legislation, and essentially master of the Budget; surely he has come to dominate the legislative process in matters relating to foreign affairs — in regulation of trade and commerce, in spending for foreign purposes, in declaring or not declaring war. Foreign policy is even more "indivisible" than is domestic policy, and what Congress does is intimately related to other policies which the President determines, and other activities which the President controls. Often, Congress does not have the information, and some Congressmen do not have the understanding, sophistication and interest, to support independent judgment. Inevitably, then, Congress is compelled to accept the grand design, the general direction, the mood, of Presidential

foreign policy; to depend on the information supplied by the Executive, often incomplete because of real or alleged needs of secrecy; to rely heavily on Executive expertise and judgment; to take on faith Executive assertions and assessments of the national interest. Congress could strike out on its own only with acute awareness of its uncertainties and inadequacies, of the risks to the national interest and its own institutional standing.

What is more, even with the best of will and greatest scruple by the Executive, Congress (or the Senate in its executive role) often does not come to face and consider what it is called upon to do until after the Executive and the international mills have ground long and fine. By the time Congress considers a trade bill or a provision for arms or foreign aid (or the Senate considers a treaty), negotiations have been held, understandings reached and commitments made (political if not legal), and Congress is far from free to exercise independent judgment. The result often is that the hand of Congress is forced, that it faces a *fait* virtually *accompli,* that it can only rubber-stamp or at most nibble away at the periphery of Executive proposals.

In our time, all know, there has been a dramatic and searing instance of such Presidential "imposition" on Congress in regard to Indochina. To me, charges of Presidential usurpation, even of Congressional abdication, are largely beside mark. Congress did delegate to Presidents virtual *carte blanche*, retaining little control and providing little supervision or guidance; one may hope that Congress will be substantially more responsible in the future. The question is whether Indochina reflects an essential ineffectiveness in the "system." Was it perhaps a "natural" consequence of dividing the power of conducting foreign relations and making and implementing much foreign policy (sometimes by use of force) from the power to decide for war? For the line between war and lesser uses of force is often illusive, sometimes illusory. Even when he does not use force, moreover, the President can incite other nations, or otherwise plunge, or stumble this country into war, or force the hand of Congress to declare or to acquiesce and cooperate in war. Once we are at war, moreover, Congressional control — which in my view Congress continues to have under the Constitution — is largely hypothetical. In Indochina, I believe, Congress had constitutional thority, by resolution or through the appropriations process, to terminate, confine or otherwise limit our participation. But a large majority of Congress felt it could not break with the President without jeopardizing the lives of American troops and other major national interests. In a word, the constitutional restraints on the President existed but were not effective.

Bifurcation of the power to formulate foreign policy is sometimes inefficient because there is a failure of cooperation between branches, or friction or "slippage" between them. Consider the making of international agreements. The treaty-making process has been far less troublesome than it was during the period culminating in the trauma of the Treaty of Versailles. If we have not returned — and could not return — to the original conception of the Senate as an advisory council participating in treaty-making at all stages, from early in the process, we have come some way towards that conception by sub-constitutional devices. Individual Senators sometimes participate in treaty negotiation; leaders or key committee members are consulted informally, so that probable Senate attitudes can be better anticipated. The process is less effective as regards multilateral treaties where the U.S. often participates in negotiation without clear intention of adhering to the treaty. And for some such treaties and some "undramatic" bilateral treaties, it is not always possible to obtain a "reading" on probable Senate attitudes. The principal ineffectiveness in regard to international agreements derives from the fact that the President alone decides which agreements should have Senate consent, that the decision to make an agreement on the President's sole authority is made essentially without Senate participation, without standards, without review.

The process for appointing ambassadors and other foreign service officers, as well as other officials who participate in formulating or implementing foreign policy, has not produced much dissatisfaction. Perhaps its chief "ineffectiveness" is that the Senate has been virtually a "rubber-stamp," with an occasional "rebellion" largely fortuitous and capricious. There are no known qualifications for appointment, or criteria for Senate approval or disapproval.

A recurrent "inefficiency" derives from the accepted constitutional view that Congress may exercise its powers in disregard of treaties or other international obligations, and the courts must give effect to the later statute: compare the Byrd Amendment dishonoring the UN embargo on Rhodesian chrome. (The counterpart, that a treaty should be applied in the face of an earlier inconsistent statute, may also be inefficient but is less troubling to foreign relations.) Presidents have also found burdensome, and interfering, Congressional control over the Executive foreign-affairs bureaucracy. Assuming the constitutional validity of legislative veto, a President would doubtless deem it an unnecessary and ineffective means for terminating authority delegated to him. Though neither Presidents nor Congresses are likely to object, some will see an unnecessary "ineffectiveness" in extravagant Congressional delegations to the President.

There is doubtless purposeful slippage and friction in that separation of powers which requires the President to go to Congress for appropriations and legislation to implement his policies. Even if I am correct in my view that constitutionally Congress is obliged to implement what the President is constitutionally entitled to formulate, the system enables Congress to challenge Presidential assertions of authority and to scrutinize what he claims he needs as implementation. But the President may have legitimate objection to being subjected to the maddening inefficiency of a two-tier authorization and appropriation process, and to the occasional abuse of that process for scrutiny and even harassment of officials in regard to matters not relevant to the subject at hand.

III. THE QUEST FOR REMEDIES

Assuming that I have correctly identified and diagnosed the inefficiencies in our system for formulating and implementing foreign policy, regretfully I have no sure remedies to offer, only some hesitant views about directions and means to explore.

Should the Constitution Be Amended?

To begin, I do not consider promoting effectiveness by constitutional amendment which would eliminate or substantially modify the separation of powers. There are good arguments against separation, particularly in foreign affairs; surely, even among western democracies sharing our political values, our separation is unique. There are good arguments against our particular separations: the intended division of policy making between the treaty-makers and the law-makers did not anticipate how the country would develop, and how the institutions – the Presidency, the Senate, the Congress – would develop; the larger division of foreign-policy-making between President and Congress which we now have, probably was not intended at all. But major changes as regards foreign affairs do not command wide agreement or support, and would not be achieved readily, if at all; they could not be achieved without a major transformation of our system of government generally. This is not the occasion and the context for considering whether the United States should convert, say, to the parliamentary system. (I indulge only the comment that a parliamentary system could not be the answer for those whose objection has been that the President has too much power and Congress not enough; in contemporary parliamentary systems generally, the prime minister with a majority in parliament has virtually unlimited constitutional power, and the parliament virtually none.)

I address the question of remedies, then, on the assumption that our system for formulating and implementing foreign policy is not so ineffective as to call for radical revision of our system of government; that the uses and values of separation are not exhausted; that they apply also in foreign affairs, although in different ways and degrees; that the more effective system we seek assumes essential continuity with our past, and while it may require institutional changes, these should be sought without sacrificing essential separation and other constitutional values. Some might suggest, indeed, that what we seek are means to make separation more effective.

In other respects, too, I do not see the "more effective system" in constitutional amendment. Our Constitution has not had major amendment: since the original ten amendments, which were the condition of ratification and essentially part of the "original package," the Constitution has been significantly, structurally amended only in the wake of the Civil War. Instead, issues have been resolved and changes – radical as well as incremental – effected by political interpretation confirmed in political battle and accommodation, sometimes also in judi-

cial interpretation. Effectively, moreover, the only method for amending the Constitution requires – to begin with – a two-thirds majority in both House and Senate; when that majority is available for change, it can achieve much for our purposes without formal amendment.

Thus, the struggle that was required, even after Vietnam and "Watergate," to adopt the War Powers Resolution, suggests that unsettled issues of Presidential authority to use force short of war, or the right of Congress to control his conduct of war, could not be happily settled by constitutional amendment; surely, one might wait to see the results of that resolution, and of Vietnam, and of "Watergate," before considering amendment. Similarly, we do not need another round of "Bricker Amendments" to define the proper scope of sole executive agreements: there is not agreement on what the line between treaties and Presidential agreements should be, and I do not think it can be nicely contained in a formula; certainly one ought not now lock some untried formula into the Constitution. Or, while I would prefer that Congress not be free to legislate in disregard of our international obligations, I doubt that a constitutional amendment to that effect could be adopted; and Congress could eliminate that issue in practice simply by legislating responsibly in the face of international obligations. Again, we should not (as is frequently suggested) amend the Constitution to require consent to a treaty by both House and Senate. The Senate, whose approval is required (in the principal procedure for amending the Constitution), is not likely to agree to deprive itself of its privileged status. Such a change, moreover, would not make our treaty process "more effective." And our existing system allows an equal role for the House whenever the Senate is willing to have an international agreement approved by joint resolution of Congress (instead of by the Senate as a treaty).

The issues of separation which trouble all Congressional-Executive relations, foreign and domestic, also do not cry for resolution by constitutional amendment. Congresses and Presidents both recognize that there must be some Executive privilege, but not too much; how much is too much is not agreed, and probably could not be generalized into a constitutional formula. The courts, I expect,

ll continue to shape and limit the scope of
executive privilege in principle, and political forces
ll attenuate and constrain it in practice. Both
anches have been generally careful not to press
o hard, and political forces will be generally
fective to check gross excesses. (I exclude here the
re, unprecedented complex, "Watergate.")

Some of the abiding issues that might be
solved by amendment, I add, are being resolved by
e courts, *e.g.*, the President's alleged authority to
pound funds. The courts have expanded the
ncept of "standing" to permit new issues to come
fore them, and have reduced the obstacle of
olitical question." Even the validity of the Presi-
nt's use of force has been considered in lower
urts. I do not expect the courts to limit Presi-
ntial power when Congress has delegated it and
n terminate it, or when Congress otherwise claims
e power to curb the President but will not
ercise it. But if Congress acts to assert authority
d "supremacy," the courts, I expect, will general-
consider and decide the issue, usually upholding
ngress. (With one exception — *Myers v. United
ites,* involving an attempt by Congress to limit the
esident's power to remove a postmaster — when-
er the President has acted inconsistently with
at Congress had prescribed, the courts have ruled
ainst the President.)

stitutional Remedies

The search for greater effectiveness, I believe,
ust look to additional understandings, formal and
formal, between the President and Congress, and
changes in organization and procedures within
oth the Executive and Legislative Branches, as well
for the conduct of relations between them. The
ganizations and procedures to be explored might
al with Presidential-Congressional relations gener-
y, with foreign affairs in particular, or with
ecific issues.

At a time when the sense of a need for
provement is strong, and resistance to change is
eakened by national malaise and political crisis, it
ight be desirable for Congress and the President —
rhaps a new Congress and a new President — to
ter "negotiations" with a view to putting their
lations generally on a cooperative, less distrustful,
ss adversary basis, not in order to mute separation
it to make it work better; to attempt to resolve, or
ake it easier to live with, issues of constitutional

principle, singly or in a package deal; to experiment
with new institutional forms and new procedures as
regards foreign relations in general as well as in
particular issues.

One might begin with a pervasive problem in
foreign affairs, secrecy, and its effect on the ability
of Congress to perform its constitutional functions.
I do not refer to Executive privilege, which has not,
in my view, been a major difficulty, but to
unnecessary secrecy in foreign relations, a significant obstacle to an effective foreign policy system
as well as to public awareness and understanding. (If
unnecessary secrecy in foreign affairs were reduced,
the significance of Executive privilege would also be
substantially smaller.) I have no illusion that, even
with the best of good will, unnecessary secrecy can
be easily reduced, but it is time to try again, and
harder. It may require new legislation by Congress,
new regulation by the President, new machinery
within the Executive Branch and beyond it — to
overhaul the classification system, to set a higher
threshold for secrecy, to impose tight limitations on
authority to classify information, to establish a
system of automatic declassification, presumptions
against continued classifications, and frequent review of classifications, perhaps by a body which
includes Congressional and public representation.

There will still be the obstacle of *necessary*
secrecy in foreign affairs, the need of Congress for
access to classified information, and to a mass of
other information which is not secret but is not in
fact available to Congress. The principal "inefficiency" in our system, I have said, is the distorting
effect on the Congressional function resulting from
the President's monopoly of information and communication, and his exclusive control of the daily
conduct of foreign relations. For that major sys-
temic "defect" remedies are very difficult to con-
coct. What needs to be done is for Congress to
organize itself and establish channels to and within
the Executive Branch, so that, to the maximum
extent feasible, Congress — through selected individuals or committees representing it — will be
effectively informed; will have the sense of our
foreign policy and our foreign relations in gross and
in important detail; will be aware of attitudes as
they are being formed and commitments as they are
being made; will be able to inject Congressional
influence early, at least earlier, in matters on which

it has constitutional responsibilities, especially those on which it will have to take formal action.

One can attempt such arrangements piecemeal in regard to particular matters. I have mentioned a Congressional role in declassification. An area of obvious need is in decisions involving the use of force. Some have suggested a joint Congressional Committee, or a hybrid Executive-Congressional committee, to act as a council on war and lesser uses of force, with continuing concern also for situations which might foreseeably lead to United States military involvement.

A similar arrangement might attenuate difficulties with executive agreements. The Senate resolution requiring that executive agreements be reported to the Senate (or, if classified, to the two foreign affairs committees) will inevitably influence Presidents as to what agreements they will conclude on their own authority. But perhaps the Senate, at least, ought to have some entry into the process before agreements are concluded, before they are even well along the way. Can there be a committee or council on international agreements and international political commitments, working closely with the Executive, which might advise at least as regards formal agreements or commitments, and advise also as to which agreements should go to the Senate or to both Houses for consent?

Perhaps, even, it is time to experiment with new kinds of liaison across the board of foreign relations. The Executive Branch has for some time had officials for Congressional relations; is there a way of reversing the process so that Congress will send into the Executive Branch eyes and ears and a Congressional voice? How would it be if a small, select group — members of Congress or staff — had access to the cablegrams, attended Executive meetings, participated in discussions? Or if there were a special Executive-Legislative council on foreign affairs meeting regularly?

Let me be clear. Any novel arrangements, whether in a specific area or in regard to foreign relations generally, would be very difficult to achieve. If a recently-battered Executive Branch might be persuaded to experiment with it, it would take continued effort to keep it alive. Even more difficult to achieve, perhaps, would be the organization, effort, dedication and unusual responsibility by Congress to make it work. Congress would have

to repose full faith and credit in the few individuals legislators or staff, selected for the role; classified information and executive confidentiality would have to be scrupulously observed; the special machinery and process would have to be carefully protected from partisan politics and from abuse for partisan purposes.

Cooperation-in-Separation

New organizational machinery, even if it could be established, will not be enough. New attitudes, necessary to bring about such arrangements, will have to achieve also self-policing, in both Branches, and other forms of cooperation running from Congress to the Executive as well as from Executive to Congress.

Consider the most dramatic case, the War Powers issues. There has been much debate as to the President's authority to deploy troops, and to engage them in hostilities short-of-war, when Congress is silent; and Congress purported to define that authority in the War Powers Resolution. But that issue, I believe, is largely academic: Presidents cannot deploy troops for very long without the consent or acquiescence of Congress, indeed it active cooperation by appropriating funds and by other forms of implementation. The real issue, then is not the President's authority when Congress is silent, but whether Congress can deny or control his authority. In the War Powers Resolution, Congress purported to regulate that authority. President Nixon declared that Resolution to be unconstitutional (as well as dangerous), and future Presidents are not likely to be more hospitable to it as doctrine; neither are future Congresses likely to retreat from it in principle.

But nothing in that Resolution prevents Presidents and Congress from acting together in future cases. Indeed, in my view, the Resolution is important only as a promise of new attitudes in future Presidents have been warned to seek Congressional approval for future uses of force, and to be forthcoming and forthright in seeking it. In future then, we are entitled to expect that Congress will be honestly informed, and new forms of inter-Branch liaison of the kind I have suggested would help assure that Congress is informed fully and in time But will Congress accept the responsibility of decision, and maintain continuing and meaningful participation and control?

New forms of liaison giving Congress continuous participation would also reduce inefficiencies in the "advice-and-consent" role of the Senate, and Congressional implementation of foreign policy. There will be less excuse for rubber-stamping treaties or appointments. There will be less excuse, on the other hand, for Congressional resistance and inefficiency in appropriating funds, or for abusing the appropriation process for unrelated scrutiny of the Executive.

Continuing participation would also reduce the temptation for excessive delegations of authority and therefore the need for unusual devices to control or terminate them. The attempt by Congress to terminate delegations to the President by sub-legislative means not subject to Presidential veto (concurrent resolution, committee actions), might be reduced if not eliminated. It is not clear that this device responds to proven needs — that Presidents have in fact often vetoed (or threatened to veto) legislation discontinuing a delegation. Congress can, moreover, avoid the entire issue by delegating authority for a fixed time or until some event happens. If Presidents are unhappy with such automatic terminations, and prefer unlimited delegations, they might have to commit themselves (and, effectively, their successors) not to veto a termination.

Sub-legislative scrutiny has been used also for general oversight of Executive action in foreign affairs, and the validity of such arrangements has also not been determined. That device, too, responds to inadequate communication, and reflects an adversary spirit, between Executive and Legislative Branches. The practice, the constitutional issues it raises, and political resistance to it, all might be attenuated if there were improved institutions and procedures for inter-Branch communication.

Different forms of cooperation will be required to eliminate other areas of controversy. The Supreme Court has rejected the President's asserted authority to impound funds in a domestic case, though it did not explicitly address the constitutional issue. But impoundment, too, lends itself to inter-Branch accommodation. The pressures for impoundment would be reduced if Congress had a better grasp of the range, the priorities and other implications of the national budget. (We may expect that Congress will do better pursuant to the Congressional Budget and Impounding Control Act of 1974.) In principle, surely, especially in foreign affairs, Congress ought to consider in every case the extent to which the President should have authority not to spend what has been appropriated, or to divert it to some other specified purpose.

When there is essential difference between President and Congress as to whether to spend, our system gives the final word to Congress. To some extent, however, the impoundment issue is an outgrowth of what may be, in essence, a Congressional abuse of separation, of checks and balances. A President is sometimes tempted to impound funds, or otherwise refuse to execute a Congressional enactment or condition, where he was not free to veto it at adoption because Congress added that provision as a rider to a bill which the President could not afford to veto as a whole. If Congress wished to reduce the temptation and the asserted justification of Presidents to impound, it ought not to circumvent his constitutional right to veto by "improper packaging" of legislation. Or, the price for discontinuing impoundment may be Congressional acceptance of an "item veto."

The suggestions I offer for remedies, I repeat, are highly tentative. I am confident only of the needs to which they are addressed: to establish new attitudes and forms of cooperation, running — in both directions — between Congress and the Executive; and to enable Congress to be effectively informed of American foreign relations on a continuing basis, and to participate in the process of formulating and implementing foreign policy long before it must act formally.

Separation of powers is not an adversary game. It does not imply or require that each Branch must hold the other at arm's length; it implies and requires that they work together to enable each to exercise its separate, independent judgment. It does not imply or require each Branch to try to keep information from the other; it implies and requires, rather, that each Branch should have the information it needs to exercise its separate, independent judgment. Any measures to those ends will help make separation-of-powers work, and our kind of system for formulating and implementing foreign policy more effective.

TOWARD A RESPONSIBLE AMERICAN PRESIDENCY

by Professor Philip B. Kurland
William R. Kenan, Jr. Professor
in the College and Professor of Law
University of Chicago Law School

Note: Professor Kurland has included three appendices along with his article. They follow the article and are as follows: APPENDIX A: Senate Bill 495 entitled the "Watergate Reorganization and Reform Act of 1975"; APPENDIX B: Section by Section Analysis of S. 495, prepared by the Staff of the Senate Government Operations Committee; and APPENDIX C: Letter of March 11, 1975 from Professor Kurland to Senators Ribicoff and Percy regarding S. 495.

I

I found it necessary to rewrite my paper for the Annual Chief Justice Earl Warren Conference after I received the list of participants in this Conference. The list revealed that the immediate audience is more sophisticated and knowledgeable than I am about the facts that were the subjects of my earlier draft. Certainly there is no need for me to explain the powers of the Office of Management and Budget and its ducal realms; or to speak of the way that the F.B.I. and the C.I.A. and the other national police forces, governments unto themselves, have been perverted to partisan political ends; or to detail the way that the Presidency claims a license to pick and choose among Congressional Acts those that will be enforced and those that will be ignored; or to list the legislative powers of the Second Branch as exercised through Executive Orders and Guidelines that have the force of law but are more often used to frustrate rather than to effect the legislative will. Indeed, the catalogue could get quite long.

I decided that instead of a "background paper," I should prepare a "working paper" containing suggestions and proposals for curing some malfunctions of executive power that are, in my mind inconsistent with the constitutional structure.

Article II, § 1, provides only that: "The executive power shall be vested in a President of the United States of America." From these few words, the incumbents of the office have constructed a license for power and authority that would have astounded a medieval king of England no less a Stuart or a Hanover, and their chief ministers. From Franklin Delano Roosevelt to Gerald Ford, the Presidents of the United States have found in these words an ever-broadening charter to be the sole legitimate custodian of national sovereignty. And when the origin and meaning of the words could not be construed to this end, reliance has been placed on successful usurpations by their predecessors which, like bricks and mortar, have been put together one by one to build the magnificent edifice that is "the Presidency." It is not only an edifice but a shrine, at which all of us are expected to pay homage and fealty, as most of us have in fact done.

Were it not for the series of events that took on the name Watergate, perhaps there would have been no serious question raised about this ever-increasing concentration of governmental authority. One day, perhaps, we might owe a debt to Richard M. Nixon, in the same way that our forbearers might feel obligated to King John for the Magna Carta, or to King Charles for the Bill of Rights, or to King George III for the American Constitution. As yet however, we have neither a Magna Carta nor a Bill of Rights to inhibit a repetition of the malfeasance of our own kings.

Indeed, there still are some among us who do not recognize the existence of an institutional problem, who believe that the transgressions of "the White House" and the Nixon Administration, were merely personal malefactions and that the removal and replacement of evil men has cured the difficulties. That is what we are told by such an eminent authority as the present Attorney General of the United States, who recently spoke of Watergate – without mentioning the word – as if it were a series of minor peccadilloes by slightly aberrant office holders demonstrating a few errors of judgment that had been blown out of proportion by a sensational press. Trust us, he said in effect, for we truly have your interests at heart and unless there is faith in government, government cannot function.

The last sentiment is right; it is the equation that is wrong. There must be faith in government, but there must not be an equation of government with the executive branch. And if there is to be faith in government, it will come when government proves its entitlement to that faith, a proof which is still delinquent.

Nor is it only Administration spokesmen who find in Watergate the deficiencies of men rather than institutions. Thus, Lawrence O'Brien, among other politicians, and James Reston, among other columnists, warn against limitations on the executive power simply because it has been abused. They would have us believe that the abuses were idiosyncratic to the Nixon regime and would not be repeated as long as the proper men exercised the presidential prerogative. But they do not tell us how to choose these Platonic guardians.

Perhaps they should read Ben Bradlee's book about Kennedy or, more to the point, George Reedy's morality tale, introduced by these words about the White House: "It is not that the people who compose the ménage are any worse than any other collection of human beings. It is rather that the White House is an ideal cloak for intrigue, pomposity, and ambition. No nation of free men should ever permit itself to be governed from a hallowed shrine where the meanest lust for power can be sanctified and the dullest wit greeted with reverential awe . . . . It is not enough to say that the White House need not be like this if it is occupied by another set of personalities . . . . The fact remains that the institution provides camouflage for all that is petty and nasty in human beings and enables a clown or a knave to pose as Galahad and be treated with deference." Neither Bradlee nor Reedy was speaking of Nixon.

The lesson of Watergate, for me, perhaps because it was my fear before Watergate, is that we cannot trust absolute power to any branch of government, and certainly not to that branch of government that is contained in the Executive Office of the President. And if that is the lesson, the problem is how to restore or create institutional safeguards against a monopoly of power, safeguards that the Founding Fathers thought they had written

into the Constitution but which subsequent generations have written out of it.

Of course, I do not deny Edmund Burke's dictum: "The laws reach but a little way. Constitute a government how you please, infinitely the greater part of it must depend upon the exercise of the powers which are left at large to the prudence and uprightness of ministers of state." But I prefer the more familiar admonition of the 51st Federalist: "In framing a government which is to be administered by men over men, the great difficulty lies in this: you must first enable the government to control the governed, and in the next place oblige it to control itself. A dependence on the people is, no doubt, the primary control on the government; but experience has taught mankind the necessity for auxiliary precautions."

Recent experience should certainly have taught us the necessity for auxiliary precautions, but the difficult problem is to frame those auxiliary precautions so that, while the executive is not unduly hobbled, it is sufficiently fettered to make it responsible to constitutional commands and democratic principles.

There is some irony in addressing this issue to this group, for in large measure we are truly representative of the forces that have created the imperial presidency. Some of us are members of the national legislature and it is the Congress that has both licensed executive discretion and forsaken its duties of oversight that could assure that executive power would be confined to the terms of the license. There are among us members of the Fourth Estate, and it is the "media" who have glorified the presidential office, even when they have condemned it. For they have represented it to the people as though the President was the sovereign. There are here former White House officials, who have helped to effect the arrogation of power to the executive whom they served. And then there are the members of the academy, political scientists, historians, lawyers, who have spent careers justifying continuous expansion of unrestrained executive power. Until Arthur Schlesinger's recent book, *The Imperial Presidency,* from Laski and McIlwain to Rossiter and Neustadt, from Corwin to Koenig and Burns, major figures of the academy have sanctified the concentration of power in the Presidency. *Mea culpa* could well be the motto for this Annual Chief

Justice Earl Warren Conference.

II

The real problem of the post-Watergate era, however, is not to assign blame for the creation of the imperial presidency. Nor should the objective of reform be the destruction of legitimate and necessary presidential power. Rather, the problem is to provide those "auxiliary precautions" of which Madison spoke that will make the exercise of presidential authority responsible to "We, the people." Some of these proposed "auxiliary precautions" should be the subjects for our consideration here.

The responsibility of a quadrennial election is not enough to assure such responsibility, for at least two reasons. First, the period between elections is too long, too much damage could be done to the fabric of our society between elections. Certainly this is evident from the events of Watergate and of the Vietnam War. Second, there can be no real accountability, even at an election, when the actions of the administration are shrouded in secrecy, so that the public never knows what miners and sappers have been at work at the substance of a free society. This again is a clear lesson from recent events. But some would nevertheless tinker with the presidential election process by a constitutional amendment for direct popular elections, or a constitutional amendment for national presidential primaries, or a constitutional amendment to provide for election of the Vice-President by the people rather than by the Congress when that office becomes vacant, or any combination thereof. I don't believe that any of these constitutional amendments addresses our fundamental problem.

A different constitutional proposal does address the basic issue. This would substitute a parliamentary system for the presidential system. Thus, the chief executive officer would be chosen from the legislature and would be responsible to it for his continuance in office. Administrations could be changed when the confidence of the legislature was lost or the people impressed their representatives with the need for change. Under such a change, the authority of the chief executive officer would not be reduced, indeed, it would probably be enhanced. But his responsibility would be more clearly defined.

The blueprint for such a change is to be found in Professor Charles Hardin's book, *Presidential Power and Accountability*. But this constitutional revision is a most unlikely event, even if it were a desirable one. And the proposed system could work here only if there were a real two-party system in this nation. Today there is not. The so-called national parties are faction ridden. And in a parliamentary system with a multiplicity of parties, the instability overweighs any possible gain from responsibility.

We need not, however, think of reform of the presidency in constitutional terms.

The work of the Senate Watergate Committee was ultimately overshadowed by the impeachment proceedings, the Nixon resignation, and the Ford pardon. The Committee did, however, file a lengthy report which not only detailed the facts that were uncovered by the Senate investigation but also contained a series of legislative recommendations.

Just before the close of the 93rd Congress, Senator Ervin introduced a bill based on the Committee's recommendations. It was only a gesture, for it was too late in the session to hope for serious consideration. The bill was revived, however, at the opening of the 94th Congress under the principal sponsorship of Senators Ribicoff and Percy, who were joined by Senators Metcalfe, Inouye, Montoya, Weicker, and Mondale. This bill, S. 495, is entitled the Watergate Reorganization Act of 1975. At the moment it is languishing in the Senate Government Operations Committee. And it may well rest there, for the leadership of neither party has come forth to move it toward realization. It will depend on the independents in the Senate or an outcry from the press and public to have the bill properly considered.

Following this paper is a copy of the bill and an analysis of its contents, prepared by the staff of the Senate Government Operations Committee. The bill deserves the serious attention of this Conference.

There are two provisions that are of particular interest to me, those calling for the creation of - (1) an office of Public Attorney for Congress, and (2) an office of a permanent special prosecutor. Of the two, it is the former that I think merits principal attention. My reasons are contained in a letter addressed to the Senate Government Operations

Committee, some time before I received an invitation to present this paper. That letter also follows this paper for your consideration.

Another legislative proposal of Senator Ervin's that died in the 93rd Congress seems of more dubious merit. It called for the separation of the Department of Justice from the executive branch of the government. Hearings on S. 2803 and S. 2978 were held before the Subcommittee on Separation of Powers of the Senate Judiciary Committee on March 26, 27, 28, and April 2, 1974. They are published under the title *Removing Politics from the Administration of Justice,* certainly a worthy goal.

The consensus seemed to be that the separation of the Department of Justice would be constitutionally doubtful and practically unwise. And yet the reason for the proposal is sound. When the incumbent Attorney General took the oath of office, he said: "We have lived in a time of change and corrosive skepticism and cynicism concerning the administration of justice. Nothing can more weaken the quality of life or more imperil the realization of the goals we all hold dear than our failure to make clear by word and deed that our law is not an instrument for partisan purposes and it is not to be used in ways which are careless of the higher values within all of us."

Legislation by way of a new reorganization act may be the appropriate answer to another problem of governmental irresponsibility. There is significance in the fact that the chief executive is no longer regarded as an individual but as a staff or an institution. The appropriate word is no longer "the President" but "the Presidency," which includes a very large number of individuals indeed. And once again the Watergate episode affords necessary information about the abuses that have resulted from this distortion of the constitutional concept.

There are at least two cancerous growths on the American body politic. One of these is the burgeoning power of the executive branch. The other has occurred within the executive branch itself, where power has shifted from the departments and old-line agencies to what is called "the Executive Office of the President." In fact, it is here that all government policy is made, and except for the President himself — and in the case of Mr. Ford, including the President himself — the wielders of

that power are all unelected, and with little or no responsibility to Congress except through the appropriations processes. In any event, the appropriations processes are under greater control of the Office of Management and Budget than of the Congress. Perhaps this will be changed through the new budget committees in the two Houses, but that remains to be seen.

The Executive Office of the President is made up first and foremost of "the White House," some three dozen-plus barons and their entourages, reminiscent of the "fourth branch of government" described by the historian, Bernard Bailyn, a professor at Harvard, as affording one of the primary causes of the American Revolution whose bicentenary we are now celebrating. The White House office is not really merely an enlarged version of the six presidential counselors provided for by the Reorganization Act of 1939, although its antecedents are to be found there. These offices are not merely means of communications between the President and the old-line agencies and departments. They are the overlords of the executive branch.

The White House office shares some power with other branches of the Executive Office, particularly the Office of Management and Budget, the Council of Economic Advisers, the Central Intelligence Agency, the Council on Environmental Quality, the Council on International Economic Policy, and the Federal Energy Office. It is here, in the Executive Office of the President, that "the Presidency" is to be found.

There are perhaps two ways of solving the problem of lack of responsibility of "the Presidency," of these governors of the American people. The first, which I would prefer, would be to dissolve these agencies and distribute their powers and authorities among the old-line agencies and departments which are creatures of the Congress and can be made accountable to the Congress. The second is to attempt to make these branches of the government directly responsible to Congress, although leaving them with their present authority. And among the ways to create such responsibility is to see that all the major domos in the Executive Office are required to have the approval of the Senate before they assume control of their fiefdoms.

If nonresponsibility is the basic problem, it is most seriously demonstrated by the so-called "intelligence agencies" of our government. Aside from the presidential tapes themselves, the most startling revelations of the Watergate period were the hints of the perversion of these intelligence forces into political police forces. And certainly twentieth century history suggests that the greatest threats to an open, democratic society derive from a political police and an unresponsive military.

It is of quintessential importance, therefore, that our intelligence and counterintelligence agencies be confined and restricted to the limited functions they were created to deal with. Once again we are met with the proposition that we should be satisfied that these agencies will exercise self-restraint so that no accountability is really required. But too much has been revealed of the activities of these forces to permit any confidence in that self-restraint. The very personnel of Watergate, connected as they were with the C.I.A., certainly raises doubts. And one need not treat as gospel such books as Wise & Ross', *The Invisible Government* or Marchetti & Marks', *The CIA and the Cult of Intelligence* to exacerbate those fears. Indeed, there is a work that purports to be fiction, Ward Just's *The Congressman Who Loved Flaubert,* that is sufficient to raise one's hackles.

There is, of course, at the moment a series of Congressional and Presidential investigations into the activities of the intelligence agencies. One can have no confidence in the Rockefeller Commission's efforts which, so far, have all the hallmarks of a cover-up. The Senate and House investigations have not even gotten off the ground and they are being frustrated by the refusal of the agencies to make available to Congress the data about their own activities. The cry is, as it was in Watergate, "national security." The argument is that the agencies feel that Congress cannot be trusted with the relevant data, but that Congress should trust the functionaries of the agencies.

If oversight by Congress is not to be the answer, it is hard to conceive of an answer. The present pattern of disclosure is a familiar one. Facts slip out about malfunctions within the intelligence services. First, they are denied. Next, they are grudgingly conceded. Then, there is a plea for secrecy against further revelations on the ground of "national security." One may well ask whether the interests of the nation's security as a democratic polity are more likely to be protected by openness, at least with regard to past behavior if not present activities, than to trust in the virtues of those who have proved to lack virtue.

It is only through an agile and exercised press that we have had any information about the scope of the efforts of our intelligence agencies. Grateful as we should be to the press, we must accept the fact that the press is a necessary but not a sufficient safeguard against a dreaded politicization of intelligence services.

This brings up the fact that in recent years the government cloak of secrecy has been erected into an impenetrable screen by the assertion of "executive privilege." One need not go so far as Professor Raoul Berger did, in his volume on *Executive Privilege,* to recognize that the doctrine, of recent growth, is a tool for the preclusion of the power of legislative oversight, which is the only real check on abuse of executive power. It is a real check, that is, to the extent that Congress is faithful to its task. Recent history — Watergate aside — doesn't suggest that this authority will necessarily be asserted.

Watergate has left us a legacy here, too. For the Supreme Court of the United States, in the form of a decision in *Nixon v. United States,* has created out of whole cloth a privilege of constitutional stature, a privilege apparently breachable only by the judiciary itself for the purpose of carrying on its criminal justice processes. Having created the privilege, the Court abstained from saying whether Congress could assert for its purposes the power the Court asserted for its own ends.

Again, Senator Ervin, as chairman of the Separation of Powers Subcommittee, long before the events of Watergate, had investigated the problem of executive privilege. Hearings in 1971, entitled *Executive Privilege: The Withholding of Information by the Executive,* addressed the problem of a statutory definition for a theretofore much-abused notion of secrecy. The subject of the hearings was draft bill, S. 1125, which would have defined the conditions under which the privilege could be asserted.

Since I believe that there is no basis in the Constitution for such a privilege, and since I believe that there is no warrant in the creation of such privilege by judicial fiat, and since I believe that there are times when such a privilege should exist, believe that pursuant to Congress' authority: "To make all Laws which shall be necessary and proper for carrying into Execution the foregoing Powers, and all other Powers vested by this Constitution in the Government of the United States, or in any Department or Officer thereof," a statutory definition of executive privilege and a statutory definition of the appropriate procedures is a necessary condition to the reality of responsibility of the executive branch to the people through the Congress.

III

I think that I have put on our plates for this Conference more than we can appropriately chew. The subject of executive responsibility is, of course, far too vast for resolution here. The subject is also far too important not to receive the attention of every organ of responsible scrutiny concerned with the maintenance of our democracy.

I am reminded, however, of a recent penetrating column by Russell Baker in *The New York Times Magazine* for May 25, 1975. It began with these words: "The Government is acting as if it wants a divorce. Signs of its disaffection have been multiplying ever since President Nixon said we had to be treated like children, and there is increasing evidence since the Vietnam collapse that unless we shape up soon the Government is going to pack up and move out on us, taking its talents to more deserving people elsewhere."

Baker's piece concluded, as I would conclude here: "We must be very careful about saying these things. The Government is nearing the end of its patience. It may become totally disgusted with us. We would not want the Government to pick up and leave us, would we?" Or would we?

S. 495

IN THE SENATE OF THE UNITED STATES

JANUARY 30, 1975

Mr. RIBICOFF (for himself, Mr. PERCY, Mr. METCALF, Mr. INOUYE, Mr. MONTOYA, Mr. WEICKER, and Mr. MONDALE) introduced the following bill; which was read twice and referred to the Committee on Government Operations

A BILL

To establish certain Federal agencies, effect certain reorganizations of the Federal Government, and to implement certain reforms in the operation of the Federal Government recommended by the Senate Select Committee on Presidential Campaign Activities, and for other purposes.

Be it enacted by the Senate and House of Representatives of the United States of America in Congress assembled,

That this Act may be cited as the "Watergate Reorganization and Reform Act of 1975".

TITLE I—ESTABLISHMENT OF GOVERNMENT OFFICES

OFFICE OF PUBLIC ATTORNEY

SEC. 101. (a) Title 28, United States Code, is amended by adding after chapter 37 the following new chapter:

"Chapter 38.—PUBLIC ATTORNEY

"Sec.
"581. Establishment of Office of Public Attorney.
"582. Jurisdiction.
"583. Powers.
"584. Notification to Attorney General of initiation of prosecution.
"585. Administrative provisions.

"§ 581. Establishment of Office of Public Attorney

" (a) (1) There is established as an independent establishment of the Government the Office of the Public Attorney (hereinafter referred to as the 'Office'). The Office shall be under the direction and supervision of the Public Attorney who shall be appointed in accordance with the provisions of paragraph (2).

" (2) The Chief Justice of the United States shall designate three retired courts of appeals judges to select and appoint the Public Attorney. The three retired courts of appeals judges so designated shall appoint, by and with the advice and consent of the Senate, the Public Attorney.

" (b) The Public Attorney shall serve for a term of five years and may be reappointed for one additional term. Any vacancy in the Office shall be filled in the same manner as the original appointment.

" (c) A retired judge designated by the Chief Justice to select and appoint the Public Attorney shall not, by reason of such service, receive any payment from the United States for such service. No retired judge who so participates in the selection and appointment of the Public Attorney shall participate in any trial or appellate proceedings in which the Public Attorney or any employee of the Office is a party.

" (d) No individual may serve as Public Attorney unless such individual has agreed in writing not to occupy or assume or discharge the duties of any office under the United States, vacancies in which are filled by popular election, or to accept any other employment in the Government, for a period of five years after the date on which such individual's services as Public Attorney are terminated.

"§ 582. Jurisdiction

" (a) The Public Attorney shall investigate and prosecute (1) allegations of corruption in the administration of the laws by the executive branch of the Government; (2) cases referred by the Attorney General because of actual or potential conflicts of interest; (3) criminal cases referred to him by the Federal Election Commission; and (4) allegations of violations of Federal laws relating to campaigns and elections for elective office.

" (b) The Public Attorney shall notify the Attorney General of the initiation or termination of an investigation or proceeding with respect to any matter within his jurisdiction under subsection (a) of this section. After the receipt of any such notification and while any investigation or proceedings to which any such notification relates is pending, the Attorney General shall, and shall cause other divisions of the Department of Justice to, refrain from conducting any investigation or prosecution with respect to the subject matter of such notification or any related or overlapping matter, and to refrain from taking any related action with respect thereto, except to the extent that the Public Attorney has given prior written approval thereof.

"(c) If at any time the Attorney General believes or has reason to believe that any investigation conducted under his supervision involves or is likely to involve any matter that would constitute a conflict of interest or that would otherwise fall within the jurisdiction of the Public Attorney under subsection (a) of this section, he shall promptly notify the Public Attorney thereof and of the reasons for such belief. Upon receipt of any such notification, the Public Attorney may in his discretion—

"(1) assume sole responsibility for any further conduct of such investigation;

"(2) participate with the Attorney General in any further conduct of such investigation; or

"(3) defer to the ongoing investigation under the supervision of the Attorney General in which case the Attorney General shall keep the Public Attorney fully informed as to the further progress of any such investigation.

"§ 583. Powers

"The Public Attorney shall, with respect to any matter within his jurisdiction under section 582 of this title, have full power and authority, consistent with the Constitution of the United States—

"(1) to conduct such investigation thereof as he deems appropriate;

"(2) to obtain and review such documentary, testimonial, or other evidence or information as he deems material thereto as may be available from any source, and, if in the possession of an agency of the United States (as defined in section 6001 (1) of title 18), without regard to the provisions of section 552 (b) (with the exception of paragraph (6) thereof) of title 5;

"(3) to issue appropriate instructions to the Federal Bureau of Investigation and other domestic investigative agencies of the United States (which instructions shall be treated by the heads of such agencies as if received from the Attorney General) for the collection and delivery solely to the office of the Public Attorney of information or evidence relating to such investigation, and for the safeguarding of the integrity and confidentiality of all files, records, documents, physical evidence, and other materials obtained or prepared by the Public Attorney;

"(4) to receive appropriate national security clearances;

"(5) to issue subpenas to such persons as he may deem necessary to obtain and review and initiate or defend appropriate proceedings in any court of the United States of competent jurisdiction relating to compliance with any such subpena;

"(6) to conduct proceedings before grand juries;

"(7) to make application to any court of the United States of competent jurisdiction in a manner consistent with part V of title 18 for a grant of immunity to any witness;

"(8) to frame, sign, and file criminal indictments and informations, and prosecute criminal proceedings in the name of the United States, which proceedings shall, except as otherwise provided for in this chapter, comply with the requirements of law governing the conduct of such proceedings;

"(9) to conduct such civil proceedings as he may deem appropriate to enforce any provision or obtain any remedy for violation of any law he is charged with enforcing; and

"(10) notwithstanding any other provision of law, to exercise all other powers as to the conduct of criminal investigations, prosecutions (including prosecutions for prejury committed in the course of any investigation or judicial or legislative hearing with respect to any matter within his jurisdiction), civil proceedings, and appeals, within his jurisdiction, that would otherwise be vested exclusively in the Attorney General and the United States attorney under the provisions of chapters 31 and 35 of this title and any regulation promulgated pursuant to either such chapter, and act as attorney for the Government in such investigations, prosecutions, proceedings, and appeals.

"§ 584. Notification to Attorney General of initiation of prosecution

"(a) The Public Attorey may sign and file any indictment returned by a grand jury convened at his request or under his direction and may sign and file any criminal information, with respect to any matter within his jurisdiction under section 582 of this title, except that in each such instance the Public Attorney shall give the Attorney General five days' prior written notice thereof.

"(b) If the Attorney General of the United States disapproves the filing of any indictment or information, or any subsequent action or position taken by the Public Attorney in the course of any judicial proceeding pursuant thereto, the Attorney General shall be entitled to appear and present his views amicus curiae to any court before which any such proceeding is pending.

"§ 585. Administrative provisions

"(a) The Public Attorney may appoint, fix the compensation, and assign the duties of such personnel as may be necessary to carry out his duties and functions under this chapter. The Public Attorney may obtain the services of experts and consultants in accordance with the provisions of section 3109 of title 5.

"(b) The Public Attorney may from time to time make such provisions as he considers appropriate authorizing the performance by any other officer or employee of the Office of any function of the Public Attorney.

"(c) The Public Attorney is authorized—

"(1) to adopt, amend, and repeal such rules and regulations as may be necessary to carry out his duties and functions under this chapter; and

"(2) to utilize, with their consent, the services, equipment, personnel, and facilities of any department or agency of the United States on a reimbursable basis.

"(d) The Public Attorney may, in his discretion, appoint special assistants to discharge his responsibilities with respect to a particular matter or matters within his jurisdiction.

"(e) Upon request made by the Public Attorney each Federal department and agency is authorized and directed to make its services, equipment, personnel, facilities, information (including suggestions, estimates, and statistics) available to the greatest practicable extent consistent with the laws, to the Public Attorney in the performance or his duties and functions.".

(b) Section 202 of title 18, United States Code, is amended by redesignating subsection (b) as subsection (c) and adding after subsection (a) the following new subsection:

"(b) As used in sections 205, 207, 208, and 209 of this title the term 'officer or employee' includes the Public

Attorney and members of his staff; and as used in section 201 of this title the term 'public official' includes the Public Attorney and professional members of his staff.".

(c) (1) Section 1905 of title 18, United States Code, is amended—

(A) by inserting " (a) " immediately before "Whoever"; and

(B) by adding at the end thereof the following new subsection:

" (b) (1) It shall be unlawful for any officer or employee of the United States or of any department or agency thereof, or the member of any grand jury convened at the request or under the direction of the Public Attorney who, in the course or under color of his duties as such officer, employee, or member has had any direct contact with an employee or officer lawfully participating in an investigation being conducted by the Public Attorney pursuant to chapter 39 of title 28 by virtue of which such person has come into the possession of any evidence or information obtained by or in the possession of the Public Attorney or the product of an investigation conducted by the Public Attorney pursuant to such chapter, to disclose, or to cause the disclosure, or in any manner to further the disclosure, of such evidence, information, or product to any person other than an officer or employee of the Office of the Public Attorney or the Department of Justice, or of a court in which a grand jury convened at the request or under the direction of the Public Attorney is proceeding, or (to the extent otherwise provided for by law) to a person who is likely to or has become the subject of an investigation by the Public Attorney, except that the Public Attorney may make such public disclosure as is permitted by law of such information as he deems necessary, appropriate, or required by law in connection with a procedeing instituted by him.

" (2) Whoever violates any provision of paragraph (1)

of this subsection shall be subject to a civil penalty of not less than $1,000 or more than $25,000 and, if the violation is willful, shall be fined not more than $50,000 or imprisoned for one year, or both.

" (3) Nothing in this subsection shall be construed to prohibit the Public Attorney from taking any action he is authorized to take under chapter 39 of title 28, or to preclude any defendant in a criminal case from obtaining any information concerning grand jury proceedings or in the possession of a prosecuting official of the United States to which he would otherwise by law be entitled.".

(2) (A) The caption of section 1905 of such title is amended to read as follows:

"§ 1905. Disclosure of confidential information generally and with respect to investigations or proceedings conducted by the Public Attorney"

(B) The analysis of chapter 93 of such title is amended by inserting immediately before the period at the end of item 1905 the following: "and with respect to investigations or proceedings conducted by the Public Attorney".

(d) Section 5313 of title 5, United States Code, is amended by adding at the end thereof the following:

" (22) Public Attorney.".

(e) The Administrator of General Services shall provide the Office of the Public Attorney with such offices and support facilities as may be necessary, and such additional offices and support facilities as may from time to time be required to carry out the provisions of this Act, except that such offices and facilities shall be physically separate from the office of the Department of Justice or of any division thereof.

CONGRESSIONAL LEGAL SERVICE

SEC. 102. (a) For purposes of this section—

(1) "Member of Congress" means a Senator, Representative, Delegate, or Resident Commissioner;

(2) "Member of the House of Representatives" includes a Representative, Delegate, or Resident Commissioner;

(3) "State" includes any territory or possession of the United States; and

(4) "deferral of budget authority" shall have the same meaning as provided in the Congressional Budget and Impoundment Control Act of 1974 (88 Stat. 297).

(b) (1) There is established within the Congress a Congressional Legal Service, which shall be under the direction and control of the Congressional Legal Counsel. The Congressional Legal Counsel shall be appointed by the Speaker of the House of Representatives and the President pro tempore of the Senate from among recommendations submitted by the majority and minority leaders of the House of Representatives and the Senate. Such appointment shall be made without regard to political affiliation and solely on the basis of his fitness to perform the duties of his office. The Congressional Legal Counsel shall receive basic pay at the rate provided for level III of the Executive Schedule under section 5314 of title 5, United States Code.

(2) The Congressional Legal Counsel may appoint and fix the compensation of such Assistant Legal Counsels and other personnel as may be necessary to carry on the work of his office. All such appointments shall be made without regard to political affiliation and solely on the basis of fitness to perform the duties of their offices.

(3) The Congressional Legal Counsel shall promulgate for his office such rules and regulations as may be necessary to carry out the duties imposed upon him by this Act. He may delegate authority for the performance of any such duty to an officer or employee of the Congressional Legal Service. No person serving as an officer or employee of such office may engage in any other business, vocation, or employment while so serving.

(4) The Congressional Legal Counsel shall cause a seal of office to be made for his office, of such design as the Speaker of the House of Representatives and the President pro tempore of the Senate shall approve, and judicial notice shall be taken thereof.

(c) (1) It shall be the duty of the Congressional Legal Counsel—

(A) to render, upon request of either House of Congress, a joint committee of Congress, any committee of either House of Congress, at least three Senators, or twelve Members of the House of Representatives, legal opinions upon questions arising under the Constitution and laws of the United States, including but not limited to, whether—

(i) a request for information or inspection of a record or other matter under section 552 of title 5, United States Code, was properly denied by an agency of the United States Government;

(ii) a nomination, or an agreement with a foreign country or regional or international organization, should have been submitted to the Senate for its advice and consent;

(iii) an activity has been undertaken or continued, or not undertaken or continued, by the executive branch of the United States Government in violation of the law or the Constitution or without any required authorization of law;

(iv) executive privilege exists, and, if so, whether it has been properly asserted; and

(v) deferrals of budget authority have been made in accordance with law;

(B) upon the request of either House of Congress, a joint committee of Congress, any committee of either

House of Congress, at least three Senators, or at least twelve Members of the House of Representatives—

(i) to advise and to consult and cooperate with parties bringing civil actions against officers and employees of the executive branch of the United States Government or any agency or department thereof, with respect to their execution of the laws, and the Constitution of the United States; and

(ii) to intervene or appear as amicus curiae on behalf of persons making such request in any action pending in any court of the United States or of a State or political subdivision thereof, in which there is placed in issue the constitutionality or interpretation of any law of the United States, or the validity of any law of the United States, or the validity of any official proceeding of, or official action taken by, either House of Congress, a joint committee of Congress, any committee of either House of Congress, or a Member of Congress, or any officer, employee, office, or agency of the Congress;

(C) to represent, upon request, either House of Congress, a joint committee of Congress, any committee of either House of Congress, a Member of Congress, or any officer, employee, office, or agency of the Congress in any legal action pending in any court of the United States or of a State or political subdivision thereof to which such House, joint committee, committee member, officer, employee, office, or agency is a party and in which there is placed in issue the validity of any official proceeding of, or official action taken by, such House, joint committee, committee member, officer, employee, office, or agency; and

(D) if an opinion has been rendered in accordance with subparagraph (A) of this paragraph, and upon re-quest of either House of Congress, a joint committee of Congress, any committee of either House of Congress, at least six Senators, or at least twenty-four Members of the House of Representatives, to bring civil actions, without regard to the sum or value of the matter in controversy, in a court of the United States to require an officer or employee of the executive branch of the United States Government, or any agency or department thereof, to act in accordance with the Constitution and laws of the United States as interpreted in such opinion.

(2) Upon receipt of written notice from the Congressional Legal Counsel to the effect that he has undertaken, pursuant to paragraph (1) (C) of this subsection, to perform any such specified representational service with respect to any designated action or proceeding pending or to be instituted, the Attorney General shall be relieved of responsibility and shall have no authority to perform such service in such action or proceeding except at the request or with the approval of the Congressional Legal Counsel.

(d) (1) Permission to intervene or to file a brief amicus curiae under subsection (c) (1) (B) (ii) of this section shall be of right, without regard to the requirements for standing as set forth in any statutes, rules, or other requirement of standing, and may be denied by a court only upon an express finding that such intervention or filing is untimely and would significantly delay the pending action.

(2) Where an actual case or controversy exists, persons making requests under subsection (c) (1) (D) of this section shall have the right to obtain judicial review of the conduct in question without regard to the requirements for standing as set forth in any statutes, rules, or other requirement of standing.

(3) For the purpose of all proceedings incident to the trial and review of any action described by paragraph (1)

(C) of subsection (c) with respect to which the Congressional Legal Counsel has undertaken to provide representational service, and has so notified the Attorney General, the Congressional Legal Counsel shall have all powers conferred by law upon the Attorney General, any subordinate of the Attorney General, or any United States attorney.

(4) The Congressional Legal Counsel, or any attorney of his office designated by him for that purpose, shall be entitled for the purpose of performing duties imposed upon him pursuant to this section to enter an appearance in any such proceeding before any court of the United States without compliance with any requirement for admission to practice before such court, except that the authorization conferred by this subsection shall not apply with respect to the admission of any person to practice before the United States Supreme Court.

(e) All legal opinions rendered by the Congressional Legal Counsel under subsection (c) (1) (A) of this section shall be published and made available for public inspection under such rules and regulations as the Congressional Legal Counsel shall promulgate.

(f) (1) Section 3210 of title 39, United States Code, is amended—

(A) by inserting immediately after "respective terms of office" the following: "the Congressional Legal Counsel,"; and

(B) by inserting immediately before "or Legislative Counsel" the following: "Congressional Legal Counsel,"

(2) Section 3216(a) of such title is amended by inserting immediately before "and Legislative Counsel" the following: "Congressional Legal Counsel,".

AUTHORIZATION OF APPROPRIATIONS

SEC. 103. (a) There are authorized to be appropriated such sums as may be necessary to carry out the provisions of section 101 of this title.

(b) There are authorized to be appropriated to the Office of the Congressional Legal Counsel such sums as may be necessary for the performance of the duties of the Congressional Legal Counsel under section 102 of this title. Amounts so appropriated shall be disbursed by the Secretary of the Senate on vouchers approved by the Congressional Legal Counsel.

TITLE II—GOVERNMENT PERSONNEL

FINANCIAL DISCLOSURE REQUIREMENTS FOR PRESIDENT AND VICE PRESIDENT

SEC. 201. (a) An individual who holds the Office of President or Vice President at any time during the year shall file a report with the Comptroller General, not later than May 15 of the following year, containing a full and complete statement of—

(1) the amount of each tax paid by the individual, or by the individual and the individual's spouse filing jointly, for the preceding calendar year, and for purposes of this paragraph "tax" means any Federal, State, or local income tax and any Federal, State, or local property tax;

(2) the amount and source of each item of income, each item of reimbursement for any expenditure, and each gift or aggregate of gifts from one source (other than gifts received from his spouse or any member of his immediate family) received by him or by him and his spouse jointly during the preceding calendar year which exceeds $100 in amount or value, including any fee or other honorarium received by him for or in connection with the preparation or delivery of any speech or address, attendance at any convention or other assembly of individuals, or the preparation of any article or other composition for publication, and the monetary value of subsistence, entertainment, travel, and other facilities received by him in kind;

(3) the identity of each asset held by him, or by him and his spouse jointly which has a value in excess of $1,000, and the amount of each liability owed by him or by him and his spouse jointly, which is in excess of $1,000 as of the close of the preceding calendar year;

(4) any transaction in securities of any business entity by him or by him and his spouse jointly, or by any person acting on his behalf or pursuant to his direction during the preceding calendar year if the aggregate amount involved in transactions in the securities of such business entity exceeds $1,000 during such year;

(5) all transactions in commodities by him, or by him and his spouse jointly, or by any person acting on his behalf or pursuant to his directon during the preceding calendar year if the aggregate amount involved in such transactions exceeds $1,000;

(6) any purchase or sale, other than the purchase or sale of his personal residence, of real property or any interest therein by him, or by him and his spouse jointly, or by any person acting on his behalf or pursuant to his direction, during the preceding calendar year if the value of property involved in such purchase or sale exceeds $1,000; and

(7) any expenditure made by another individual for the personal benefit of him or his spouse.

(b) Reports required by this section shall be in such form and detail as the Comptroller General may prescribe.

(c) All reports filed under this section shall be maintained by the Comptroller General as public records, which, under such reasonable rules as he shall prescribe, shall be available for inspection by members of the public.

(d) As used in this section—

(1) The term "income" means gross income as defined in section 61 of the Internal Revenue Code of 1954.

(2) The term "security" means security as defined in section 2 of the Securities Act of 1933 (15 U.S.C. 77b).

(3) The term "commodity" means commodity as defined in section 2 of the Commodity Exchange Act (7 U.S.C. 2).

(4) The term "transactions in securities or commodities" means any acquisition, holding, withholding, use, transfer, or other disposition involving any security or commodity.

(5) The term "immediate family" means the child, parent, grandparent, brother, or sister of an individual, and the spouses of such persons.

(e) The first report required under this section shall be filed thirty days after the date of enactment of this Act if such date occurs after May 15 of any calendar year.

PROHIBITING CAMPAIGN SOLICITATIONS BY APPOINTEES CONFIRMED BY THE SENATE AND EXECUTIVE OFFICE PERSONNEL

SEC. 202. (a) Section 7323 of title 5, United States Code, is amended to read as follows:

"§ 7323. Political contributions; prohibition

"(a) An employee in an executive agency (except an employee to whom subsection (b) of this section applies) may not request or receive from, or give to, an employee, a Member of Congress, or an officer of a uniformed service a thing of value for political purposes.

"(b) An employee in an executive agency who is appointed by the President, by and with the advice and consent of the Senate, or is paid from the appropriation for the Executive Office of the President may not request or receive from anyone a thing of value for political purposes at any time while he is such an employee and for a one-year period occurring immediately after each time he is no longer so employed.

"(c) An employee who violates this section shall be removed from the service.".

(b) Section 602 of title 18, United States Code, is amended—

(1) by inserting the subsection designation "(a)" immediately before "Whoever"; and

(2) by inserting at the end thereof the following:

"(b) Any officer or employee of the United States who requests or receives from anyone a thing of value for political purposes in violation of section 7323(b) of title 5 shall be fined not more than $5,000 or imprisoned not more than three years or both.".

APPLICATION OF HATCH ACT TO DEPARTMENT OF JUSTICE

SEC. 203. Section 7324(d) of title 5, United States Code, is amended—

(1) by inserting in clause (2), immediately after "Executive department", the following: "(other than the Department of Justice)"; and

(2) by inserting in clause (3), immediately after "an employee", the following: "who is (A) not an employee of the Department of Justice, and (B)".

INTELLIGENCE ACTIVITIES BY PERSONNEL OF THE EXECUTIVE OFFICE OF THE PRESIDENT

SEC. 204. (a) Chapter 2 of title 3, United States Code, is amended by adding at the end thereof the following:

"§ 112. Investigative and intelligence functions

"Any individual who is employed by or detailed to any agency of the Executive Office of the President, including the White House Office, who is compensated from appropriated funds, shall not, directly or indirectly, engage in any investigative or intelligence gathering activity concerning national or domestic security unless specifically authorized to do so by statute.".

(b) The analysis of such chapter is amended by adding at the end thereof the following new item:

"112. Investigative and intelligence functions.".

INTERFERENCE WITH ELECTIONS BY GOVERNMENT EMPLOYEES

SEC. 205. (a) Section 595 of title 18, United States Code is amended—

(1) by striking out "loans or grants" in the first paragraph and inserting in lieu thereof the following: "loans, grants, subsidies, or any other payments, including payments made under a contract,"; and

(2) by striking out "$1,000" and "one year" in the first paragraph and inserting in lieu thereof "$25,000" and "five years", respectively.

(b) Section 600 of such title is amended by striking out "$1,000" and "one year" and inserting in lieu thereof "$25,000" and "five years", respectively.

DISCLOSURE OF REQUEST FOR TAX AUDIT

SEC. 206. (a) Subchapter A of chapter 78 of the Internal Revenue Code of 1954 (relating to examination and inspection) is amended by redesignating section 7609 as 7610, and by inserting after 7608 the following new section:

"§ 7609. Disclosure of certain requests for investigations

"(a) General rules.

"As soon as is practical after the beginning of each calendar year, the Secretary or his delegate shall make a report to the Committee on Ways and Means of the House of Representatives, the Committee on Finance of the Senate. and the Joint Committee on Internal Revenue Taxation which describes each request, direct or indirect, received by the Secretary or his delegate during the preceding calendar year from an officer, including the President, or employee of the Executive Office of the President, including the White House Office, for information or an investigation with respect to the liability for tax of any taxpayer. Such report shall include—

" (1) the name and office of each officer or employee who makes such a request,

" (2) the name of the taxpayer who is the subject of each request, and

" (3) a description of any action which the Secretary or his delegate took with respect to such taxpayer as a result of such request.

"(b) Requests from Executive Office of the President.

"All such requests made by the President or an officer or employee of the Executive Office of the President, including the White House Office, shall be in writing and shall be maintained on file by the Secretary.

"(c) Limitation of information disclosure.

"Pursuant to such requests, the Secretary shall disclose only the name of a person or group and the general nature of an investigation if he determines that further disclosure will prejudice the rights of the person or group or the effective and impartial administration of this title."

(b) The table of sections for such subchapter A is amended by striking out the item relating to section 7609 and inserting in lieu thereof the following:

"Sec. 7609. Disclosure of certain requests for investigation.
"Sec. 7610. Cross references.".

ACCESS TO TAX RETURNS

SEC. 207. Section 6103 (a) of the Internal Revenue Code of 1954 (relating to publicity of returns and disclosure of information as to persons filing income tax returns) is amended by—

(1) striking out "upon order of the President and" and "approved by the President" in paragraph (1),

(2) striking out "the President" in paragraph (2)

and inserting in lieu thereof "the Secretary or his delegate", and

(3) adding at the end thereof the following new paragraph:

" (4) Except as provided in section 7609 (relating to disclosure of certain requests for investigations), returns referred to in paragraphs (1) and (2) shall not be open to inspection or examination by the President, the Vice President, or any officer or employee of the Executive Office of the President.".

TITLE III—CONGRESSIONAL ACTIVITIES

JURISDICTION TO HEAR CERTAIN CIVIL ACTIONS
BROUGHT BY THE CONGRESS

SEC. 301. (a) Chapter 85 of title 28, United States Code, is amended by adding at the end thereof the following new section:

"§ 1364. Congressional actions

" (a) The District Court for the District of Columbia shall have original jurisdiction, without regard to the sum or value of the matter in controversy, over any civil action brought by either House of Congress, any committee of such House, or any joint committee of Congress, to enforce or secure a declaration concerning the validity of any subpena or order issued by such House or committee, or by any subcommittee of such committee, to any officer, including the President and Vice President, or any employee of the executive branch of the United States Government to secure the production of information, documents, or other materials.

" (b) Either House of Congress, any committee of such House authorized by such House to bring suit, or any joint committee of Congress authorized by Congress to bring suit, in addition to any other available remedies, may commence and prosecute a civil action under subsection (a) in its own name or in the name of the United States in the District Court for the District of Columbia to enforce or secure a declaration concerning the validity of any subpena or order issued by such House or committee, or by any subcommittee of such committee, against any officer, including the President and Vice President, or any employee of the executive branch of the United States Government to secure the production of information, documents, or other materials.

"(c) Any House or committee commencing or prosecuting an action pursuant to this section may be represented in such action by such attorneys as it may designate.".

(b) The analysis of such chapter 83 is amended by adding at the end thereof the following new item:
"1364. Congressional actions.".

PERJURY BEFORE CONGRESSIONAL COMMITTEES

SEC. 302. (a) Section 1621 of title 18, United States Code, is amended by adding at the end thereof the following new sentence: "It is not a defense to an action brought under this section that the statement or declaration was made at a time when a quorum of the tribunal, where such tribunal is both Houses or either House of Congress, any committee or subcommittee of either House of Congress, or any joint committee, or subcommittee thereof, of Congress was not present if the oath was properly administered and taken.".

(b) (1) Section 1623 of title 18, United States Code is amended—

(A) once in subsection (a), twice in subsection (c), and once in subsection (d) by inserting immediately after "ancillary to" the following: "the Congress or to"; and

(B) by adding at the end thereof the following new subsection:

"(f) As used in this section, 'proceeding before or ancillary to the Congress' includes a proceeding before both Houses or either House of Congress, any committee or subcommittee of either House of Congress, or any joint committee, or subcommittee thereof, of Congress.".

(2) The caption of such section is amended by inserting "Congress or a," immediately after "before".

(3) The analysis of chapter 79 of such title is amended by inserting "Congress or a," immediately after "before" in item 1623.

TESTIMONY BEFORE SENATE COMMITTEES

SEC. 303. Section 133A (b) of the Legislative Reorganization Act of 1946, as amended (2 U.S.C. 190a-1 (b)), is amended to read as follows:

"(b) Each hearing conducted by each standing, select, or special committee of the Senate (except the Committee on Appropriations) shall be open to the public except (1) when the committee determines that the testimony to be taken at that hearing may relate to a matter of national security, may tend to reflect adversely on the character or reputation of the witness or any other individual, or may divulge matters deemed confidential under other provisions of law or Government regulation, or (2) when the committee determines that the requirements of efficient and productive investigation require that the meeting be closed and that the investigation would be materially harmed if a regimen of confidentiality were not imposed. Whenever any such hearing is open to the public, that hearing may be broadcast by radio or television, or both, under such rules as the committee may adopt."

TITLE IV—FEDERAL ELECTION CAMPAIGN ACTIVITIES, CONTRIBUTIONS, AND CRIMINAL SANCTIONS

FEDERAL TAX INCENTIVES FOR CAMPAIGN CONTRIBUTION

SEC. 401. (a) (1) Section 41 (a) of the Internal Revenue Code of 1954 (relating to contributions to candidates for public office) is amended by striking out "one-half" and inserting in lieu thereof "the sum".

(2) Section 41 (b) (1) of such Code (relating to maximum credit) is amended to read as follows:

"(1) MAXIMUM CREDIT.—The credit allowed by subsection (a) for a taxable year is limited to $25 ($50 in the case of a joint return under section 6013).".

(3) (A) Section 218 of such Code (relating to deduction for contributions to candidates for public office) is repealed.

(B) The table of sections for part VII of subchapter B of chapter 1 of such Code is amended by striking out the item relating to section 218 and inserting in lieu thereof the following:

"Sec. 218. Repealed.".

(b) The amendments made by this section apply to contributions made after December 31, 1974.

PENALTY FOR ILLEGAL CAMPAIGN CONTRIBUTIONS

SEC. 402. The second paragraph of section 610 of title 18, United States Code, is amended by striking out all after the first semicolon and inserting in lieu thereof the following: "and every officer or director of any corporation, or officer of any labor organization, who consents to any contribution or expenditure by the corporation or labor organization as the case may be, and any person who accepts or receives any contribution, in violation of this section, shall be fined not more than $50,000 or imprisoned not more than two years, or both.".

UNLAWFUL USE OF CAMPAIGN MATERIALS

SEC. 403. (a) Section 612 of title 18, United States Code, is amended—

(1) by inserting "(a)" immediately before the text of such section; and

(2) by adding at the end thereof the following new subsection:

"(b) Whoever embezzles, steals, or by fraud or deception obtains from any individual who has publicly declared his intent to seek nomination for election, or election, to any Federal office in an election or has caused or permitted his intention to do so to be publicly declared, any campaign materials, documents, or papers which are not available for public dissemination and which belong to, or are in the custody of, any such person shall be fined not more than $5,000, or imprisoned not more than five years, or both.".

(b) (1) The caption of such section is amended by adding at the end thereof the following: "and theft of campaign materials".

(2) The analysis of chapter 29 of such title is amended by inserting immediately before the period in the item relating to section 612 a semicolon and the following: "unlawful use of campaign materials.".

CRIMINAL SANCTIONS GENERALLY

SEC. 404. (a) Chapter 29 of title 18, United States Code, is amended by adding at the end thereof the following new sections:

"§ 618. Use of funds to finance violation of provisions of Federal election laws

"No person may make any expenditure, payment of money, or transfer of other property to compensate another person for violating any provision of this chapter or of any other law of the United States relating to elections, or to compensate any other person for engaging in any activity which the individual making the expenditure, payment, or transfer knows, or has reason to know, will probably result in a violation of any such provision. Violation of the provisions of this section is punishable by a fine of not to exceed $25,000, imprisonment for not to exceed five years, or both.

"§ 619. Contributions by certain other recipients of Federal funds

"(a) No person who receives one or more grants, loans, or subsidy payments in excess of $5,000, singly or in the aggregate, in any calendar year from funds appropriated by the Congress may make a contribution during that year to any other person for any political purpose. No person may solicit a contribution from any person to whom the preceding sentence applies during any calendar year during which he is prohibited, on account of the application of such sentence, from making a contribution.

"(b) For purposes of this section, each officer or director of a corporation which receives such grants, loans, or other subsidy payments is considered to have received the entire amount of grants, loans, or other subsidy payments received by the corporation during the calendar year.

"(c) Violation of the provisions of this section is punishable by a fine of not more than $5,000, imprisonment for not more than five years, or both.".

"§ 620. Fraudulent infiltration of Federal election campaigns for espionage and sabotage purposes

"Whoever—

"(1) obtains employment, voluntary or paid, in a campaign of any person who has publicly declared his intent to seek nomination for election, or election, to Federal office in any election by false pretenses, misrepresentation, or any other fraudulent means for the purpose of interfering with, spying on, or obstructing any campaign activity of such person; or

"(2) causes any person to obtain employment, voluntary or paid, in any such campaign for such purpose; shall be fined not more than $5,000, or imprisoned not more than five years, or both.

"§ 621. Misrepresentation of a candidate for elective office

"Whoever willfully makes any false, fictitious, or fraudulent statements or representations that such person represents any person who has publicly declared his intention to seek nomination for election, or election, to Federal office in any election or has caused or permitted his intention to do so to be publicly declared, for the purpose of interfering with any such election, shall be fined not more than $5,000, or imprisoned for not more than five years, or both.

"§ 622. Crimes affecting elections

"(a) It constitutes a separate offense and a violation of this section for a person to commit a violation of any provision of State law or of any provision of this title, other than any other provision of this chapter, if the violation—

"(1) was committed for the purpose of interfering with, or affecting the outcome of, an election, and

"(2) is punishable by imprisonment for more than one year.

"(b) Violation of the provisions of subsection (a) is punishable by a fine not to exceed $25,000, imprisonment for not more than five years, or both.".

(b) (1) Section 591 of title 18, United States Code, as amended by section 404 (b) (1) of this Act is amended by striking out "and 613" and inserting in lieu thereof "612, 613, 614, 615, 616, 617, 618, 619, 620, 621, and 622".

(2) The table of sections for chapter 29 of title 18, United States Code, is amended by adding at the end thereof the following new items:

"618. Use of funds to finance violation of provisions of Federal election laws.
"619. Contributions by certain other recipients of Federal funds.
"620. Fraudulent infiltration of Federal election campaigns for espionage and sabotage purposes.
"621. Misrepresentation of a candidate for elective office.
"622. Crimes affecting elections.".

OBSTRUCTION OF GOVERNMENT FUNCTIONS

SEC. 405. (a) Chapter 47 of title 18, United States Code, is amended by adding at the end thereof the following new section:

"§ 1028. Obstruction of Government functions generally

"Whoever intentionally obstructs, impairs, or perverts a Government function by defrauding the Government of the United States, or any department or agency thereof, in any manner, shall be fined not more than $10,000 or imprisoned not more than five years, or both.".

(b) The analysis of such chapter is amended by adding at the end thereof the following new item:

"1028. Obstruction of Government functions generally."

APPENDIX B

WATERGATE REORGANIZATION AND REFORM ACT OF 1975
SECTION BY SECTION ANALYSIS
(Prepared By the Staff of the Senate Government Operations Committee)

TITLE I:
ESTABLISHMENT OF GOVERNMENTAL OFFICES

Public Attorney

Section 101(a) amends title 28, United States Code, by inserting a new chapter 39, which consists of five new sections, as follows:

New section 581 establishes an independent Office of Public Attorney under the direction of a Public Attorney appointed, with the advice and consent of the Senate, by a panel of three retired court of appeals judges designated by the Chief Justice. It sets a five year term for the Public Attorney, who may be reappointed once. The panel of judges shall not be paid for their service nor permitted to participate in any trial or appellate proceeding to which the Public Attorney is a party. No person shall serve as Public Attorney unless he agrees in writing not to seek or hold elective office nor accept government employment for a five year period following his term of service.

New section 582 of new chapter 39 gives the Public Attorney authority to investigate and prosecute (1) allegations of corruption in the administration of the law by the Executive branch; (2) cases referred by the Attorney General because of actual or potential conflict of interest; (3) criminal cases referred by the Federal Election Commission; and (4) allegations of violations of Federal election laws. The Public Attorney shall notify the Attorney General of the initiation or termination of any investigation or proceeding. Upon such notification, the Attorney General shall direct the Department of Justice to refrain from any related investigation or prosecution unless prior written approval has been given by the Public Attorney. The Attorney General shall notify the Public Attorney of any investigation in which he believes a conflict of interest exists or is likely to arise or which involves a matter under the jurisdiction of the Public Attorney. Upon such notification, the Public Attorney shall decide whether to accept responsibility for the investigation, participate with the Attorney General in continuing the investigation, or leave responsibility with the Attorney General, provided that the Public Attorney is kept fully informed of the progress of the investigation.

New section 583 empowers the Public Attorney to (1) conduct investigations; (2) obtain and review evidence and information; (3) instruct the Federal Bureau of Investigation and other domestic investigative agencies to collect information and evidence and to safeguard material obtained or prepared by the Public Attorney; (4) receive appropriate national security clearances; (5) issue subpoenas; (6) conduct proceedings before grand juries; (7) apply for a grant of immunity for a witness; (8) frame, sign and file criminal indictments and prosecute criminal proceedings; (9) conduct civil proceedings; and (10) exercise all other powers as to the conduct of criminal investigations, prosecutions, civil proceedings and appeals within his jurisdiction as the Attorney General would have under chapters 31 and 35 of title 28.

New section 584 requires the Public Attorney to give 5 days written notice to the Attorney General prior to signing or filing any indictment of criminal information, and it permits the Attorney General to appear as an amicus curiae if he disapproves of the Public Attorney's action.

New section 585 authorizes the Public Attorney to (a) appoint personnel; (b) delegate responsibilities; (c) adopt rules and regulations necessary to carry out his duties, and to utilize the facilities and services of other government agencies on a reimbursable basis; (d) appoint special assistants; and (e) request services, equipment, personnel, facilities and information from other Federal agencies.

Section 101(b) amends section 202 of title 18, United States Code, to include the Office of Public Attorney within the scope of the definitions contained in that section.

Section 101(c) prohibits any government officer or employee or member of a grand jury convened at the request of the Public Attorney from disclosing any evidence or information obtained by the Public Attorney to any person other than an officer or employee of the Office of Public Attorney or the Justice Department or of the court, or to a person under or likely to come under an investigation by the Public Attorney. It establishes a civil penalty of $1,000 to $25,000 fine for violations, and a fine of not more than $50,000 or five years imprisonment or both for willful violations.

Section 101(d) amends section 5313 of title 5, United States Code to include the term "Public Attorney."

Section 101(e) directs the Administrator of General Services to provide the Office of Public Attorney with offices and support facilities physically separate from the Department of Justice.

Congressional Legal Service

Section 102(a) defines (1) "Member of Congress" to mean a Senator, Representative, Delegate or Resident Commissioner; (2) "Member of the House of Representatives" to mean any territory or possession of the United States; and (4) "deferral of budget authority" to mean the same as provided i the Congressional Budget and Impoundment Co: trol Act of 1974.

Section 102(b) establishes a Congression. Legal Service under the direction of a Congression. Legal Counsel to be appointed by the Speaker of the House of Representatives and the President pr tempore of the Senate from among recommend. tions submitted by the majority and minorit leaders of both Houses. The Congressional Leg. Counsel may appoint personnel, promulgate nece sary rules and regulations, and delegate authority t his employees.

Section 102(c)(1) requires the Congression. Legal Counsel to render legal opinions upon th request of either House of Congress, a joint Co. gressional Committee, a Committee of either Hous three Senators, or twelve Representatives on th following subjects: (1) whether a request for info mation or records from a government agency w. properly denied; (2) whether a nomination c agreement with a foreign country or regional c international organization should have been su mitted to the Senate for advice and consent; (3 whether the Executive branch undertook or faile to undertake an activity in violation of the law c without required legal authorization; (4) whethe executive privilege exists and was properly asserte or (5) whether budget authority was deferred i accordance with the laws. He shall also advise consult and cooperate with parties bringing civ actions against the Executive branch regarding it execution of laws, and intervene or appear as a amicus curiae in court actions questioning th validity, interpretation or constitutionality or an law or the validity of any official Congression action, upon the request of either House of Cor gress, a joint Congressional Committee, a Commi tee of either House, three Senators or twelv Representatives. He shall represent upon reques either House of Congress, a joint Committee, an Committee of either House, a Member of Congres or an officer, employee, office or agency of Cor gress in any legal action questioning the validity c any official proceeding or action taken. He sha bring civil actions, upon the request of either Hous of Congress, a joint Congressional Committee, committee of either House, six Senators or twenty four Representatives, to require the Executiv

nch to act in accordance with a legal opinion he
dered.

Section 102(c)(2) relieves the Attorney General of any representational responsibility upon itten notification from the Congressional Legal unsel that he has been requested to undertake t function.

Section 102(d) grants (1) a court the authorto disallow the filing of an amicus curiae brief or deny permission to intervene only upon finding t such action by the Congressional Legal Counsel untimely and would cause delay; (2) those rsons requesting the Congressional Legal Counsel institute a civil action the right of obtaining icial review without regard to the requirements standing; (3) the Congressional Legal Counsel the ne powers that the Attorney General would have pursuing such civil actions; and (4) the Congresnal Legal Counsel or designated attorney from Congressional Legal Service to appear before y Court, except the United States Supreme Court, gardless of court requirements for admission to actice.

Section 102(e) requires that the legal opinions dered by the Congressional Legal Counsel be blished and made available to the public.

Section 102(f) amends Sections 3210 and 16 of title 39, United States Code, to include ferences to the Congressional Legal Counsel.

TITLE II: GOVERNMENT PERSONNEL

Financial Disclosure

Section 201(a) requires the President and the ce President to file by May 15 of each year with e Comptroller General a report containing a full tement of (1) Federal, State and local income d property taxes paid; (2) the amount and source each item of income, reimbursement or gift ceeding $100 in value, including fees, honoraria, nvention attendance, entertainment, travel, and her services or facilities received in kind; (3) the entity of each asset or liability in excess of ,000; (4) any transaction in securities in excess of ,000; (5) any transactions in commodities in cess of $1,000; (6) any purchase or sale of real operty, other than a personal residence, in excess $1,000; and (7) any expenditure made by

another individual for the personal benefit of him or his spouse.

Section 201(b) authorizes the Comptroller General to prescribe the form and detail of the report.

Section 201(c) requires the Comptroller General to maintain such reports and make them available for public inspection.

Section 201(d) defines the term (1) "income" to mean gross income as defined in section 61 of the Internal Revenue Code of 1954; (2) the term "security" to mean security as defined in section 2 of the Securities Act of 1933 (15 U.S.C. 77b); (3) the term "commodity" to mean commodity as defined in section 2 of the Commodity Exchange Act (7 U.S.C. 2); (4) the term "transactions in securities and commodities" to mean any acquisition, holding, withholding, use, transfer or other disposition involving any security or commodity; (5) the term "Member of Congress" to mean a Senator, Representative, Resident Commissioner, or Delegate; (6) the term "officer" to have the same meaning as it has in section 2104 of title 5, United States Code; (7) the term "employee" to have the same meaning as it has in section 2105 of title 5, United States Code; (8) the term "uniformed service" to mean any of the Armed Forces, the commissioned corps of the Public Health Service or the commissioned corps of the National Oceanic and Atmospheric Administrations; and (9) the term "immediate family" to mean the child, parent, grandparent, brother, or sister of an individual and the spouses of such persons.

Section 201(e) establishes that the first report required under Section 201(a) shall be due within thirty days of the enactment of this Act if such date occurs after May 15 of any calendar year.

Political Contributions

Section 202(a) prohibits employees in an executive agency from requesting or receiving from, or giving to another employee, a Member of Congress or a military officer a thing of value for political purposes. Any employee of an executive agency appointed by the President with the Advice and consent of the Senate or paid from the appropriations for the Executive Office of the President may not request or receive from anyone a thing of value for political purposes while an employee and for one year thereafter. An employee who violates this section shall be removed.

Section 202(b) establishes a fine of not more than $5,000 or 3 years imprisonment or both for an officer or employee who gives, receives, or requests a thing of value for political purposes.

Extension of Hatch Act to Department of Justice

Section 203 extends the coverage of the Hatch Act to the Department of Justice, including the Attorney General.

Intelligence Activities

Section 204 prohibits employees of, or persons paid by funds appropriated to, any agency of the Executive Office of the President from engaging in any investigative or intelligence gathering activity, unless specifically authorized by statute.

Interference with Elections by Government Employees

Section 205(a) prohibits employees involved in the administration of Federal subsidies and other payments from using their official authority to influence a Federal election.

Section 205(b) amends section 600 of title 18, United States Code, relating to penalties for violations by increasing the fine that may be imposed from not more than $1,000 or 1 year imprisonment or both to not more than $25,000 or 5 years imprisonment or both.

Disclosure of Request for Tax Audit

Section 206 requires the Secretary of the Treasury to report annually to the House Committee on Ways and Means, the Senate Finance Committee, and the Joint Committee on Internal Revenue Taxation, a description of each request from an officer, including the President, or employee of the Executive Office of the President, for an investigation of a taxpayer, including the name and position of the person making the request, the name of the person to be investigated and the action taken on the request. The Secretary shall disclose only the name of a person or group and the general

nature of an investigation pursuant to such requests if he determines that further disclosure will prejudice the rights of the person or group or the effective and impartial administration of the tax laws.

Access to Tax Returns

Section 207 provides that income tax returns shall not be open to inspection by the President or officers or employees of the Executive Office of the President except pursuant to a request for an investigation or information as provided in section 206.

TITLE III: CONGRESSIONAL ACTIVITIES

Jurisdiction of Certain Civil Actions

Section 301 gives the District Court of the District of Columbia jurisdiction over civil actions brought by either House of Congress or any committee of Congress to enforce subpoenas, and authorizes Congress to initiate such actions.

Section 302 amends section 1621 of title 18, United States Code, to disallow the absence of a quorum in a Congressional committee or subcommittee as a defense against perjury.

Testimony Before Senate Committees

Section 303 permits hearings before Senate committees to be closed to the public when the committee determines that the requirements of efficient and productive investigation require that the meeting be closed and that the investigation would be materially harmed if a regimen of confidentiality were not imposed.

TITLE IV: FEDERAL ELECTION CAMPAIGN ACTIVITIES

Tax Incentives for Campaign Contributions

Section 401 increases the maximum tax credit for political contributions to $25 ($50 on a joint return) and abolishes tax deductions for political contributions.

Penalty for Illegal Contributions

Section 402 increases the penalty for illegal contributions by corporations and labor organizations, to not more than a $50,000 fine or 2 years imprisonment or both.

Unlawful Use of Campaign Materials

Section 403 prohibits the stealing of, or obtaining by deception, non-public campaign materials or documents belonging to a candidate for Federal office. Violations are punishable by a fine of not more than $5,000 or five years imprisonment, or both.

Criminal Sanctions

Section 404(a) amends Chapter 29 of title 18, United States Code, by adding the following new sections:

Section 618 prohibits the use of campaign funds to finance a violation of Federal election laws. Violations are punishable by a fine of not more than $25,000 or five years imprisonment or both.

Section 619 prohibits any person who receives a Federal grant, loan or subsidy in excess of $5,000 annually from making a political contribution. Solicitation of contributions from such persons is also prohibited. Violations are punishable by a fine of not more than $5,000 or five years imprisonment or both.

Section 620 prohibits any person from seeking or encouraging another person to seek employment in a campaign for the purpose of interfering with, spying on, or obstructing a Federal campaign. Violations are punishable by a fine of not more than $5,000 or five years imprisonment.

Section 621 prohibits any person from making false statements or misrepresentations about a candidate for nomination or election to Federal office. Violations are punishable by a fine of not more than $5,000 or five years imprisonment or both.

Section 622 establishes penalties for violations of title 18, United States Code, or of State law for the purpose of interfering with or affecting the outcome of a Federal election, of a fine of not more than $25,000 or five years imprisonment or both.

Section 404(b) amends section 591 of title 18, United States Code, and the table of sections for chapter 29 to reflect the inclusion of the new sections.

Obstruction of Government Functions

Section 405 amends chapter 47 of title 18, United States Code, by adding a new section 1028 establishing a fine of not more than $10,000 or five years imprisonment or both for obstructing a government function.

APPENDIX C

LETTER FROM PROFESSOR KURLAND
TO SENATORS RIBICOFF AND PERCY REGARDING S. 495

11 March 1975

Dear Senators Ribicoff and Percy:

I have your letter of inquiry about S. 495. I beg off trying to answer all the questions that are in your letter for several reasons. First, it would take too long to make a reasoned response to each of them within the necessary deadline. Second, if I did, my answers would probably prove to be only redundant of the other responses that you will receive to your inquiry. Third, I have a suggestion for a fundamental change in the bill which would eliminate, or at least diminish, some of the difficulties that you suggest with the bill as drafted. It is this last item that I wish to address here.

Essentially, my proposition is that the objectives to be sought through the creation of the offices of Public Attorney and Congressional Legal Counsel be combined in a single office of Congressional Legal Counsel. While this would eliminate the concept of a law officer who would proceed through the courts as a prosecutor would, I think that the objective of such an office might better be served by legislative rather than judicial processes. Moreover, I would charge the Office of Congressional Legal Counsel with one function that is not proposed in this bill.

The proposed Public Attorney is obviously patterned on the role of the Watergate Special Prosecutor. While I admire the work that Cox and Jaworski performed, I am by no means convinced that for the kinds of malfeasance they addressed, criminal trials were the best answer. They were, of course, properly ancillary to the work of the Senate Select Committee on Presidential Campaign Finances and the House Judiciary Committee's impeachment processes, but not alternatives to these efforts.

My suggestion is that the investigatory and prosecutorial function of the new Congressional Legal Counsel be confined to the legislative and impeachment processes set forth in the Constitution. As you know, impeachment is not limited to the office of the President or Vice-President, but extends to all executive branch officials, as well as the judiciary. Moreover, its function may be extended to persons who have already separated themselves or been separated from the service of the nation. If, as I believe, the primary obligation in the case of defalcation or dereliction of duty of an important official is not so much his imprisonment as publicizing the wrongdoing in order to seek legislative means of preventing its recurrence, then the legislative processes are better geared to the proper end than the judicial. And, as the impeachment provisions provide, in the event that the legislative or impeachment processes reveal criminal activity, criminal prosecutions may be brought after the legislative processes have ended, whatever conclusion the Congress may reach.

I would, therefore, suggest the creation of an office of Congressional Legal Counsel, which would be charged with the duty to investigate and prosecute misbehavior of executive and judicial officials — and legislative officials as well — either before the House Judiciary Committee, in the event of a formal impeachment process, or before an appropriate committee of either the House or Senate, where the objective is not removal but curative legislation, and before the proper legislative committee, where the question is the misbehavior of a member of the House or Senate.

For these purposes, the office would have to have all the investigative capacities which the bill proposes to make available to the Office of Public Attorney, except the power of judicial prosecution. But granting these powers as consequent upon the legislature's power of investigation and oversight would raise none of the questions of constitutionality that derive from the creation of a separate office of Public Attorney for criminal prosecutions. I should think it clear that such an official could be appointed by legislative leadership, perhaps with the approval of the Judiciary Committees, or even the approval of both Houses. I should think, too, that his contract of employment could clearly preclude him from accepting any office within five years after his retirement. Whether such a provision could be subject to specific enforcement or liquidated damages, such as the return of all his earned salary, or both, would be a matter that could be left to future resolution. I do have doubts, however, in light of the Supreme Court's decision in *Powell v. McCormack*, 395 U.S. 486 (1969), that the Congress has the authority to add to the qualifications for those offices specified in the Constitution, that is, Representatives, Senators, and President and Vice-President. A disqualification of a Congressional Counsel, for election to these offices, might be considered to add such an invalid qualification.

I should add that I think that the Office of Congressional Counsel should have, as well as the functions I have suggested above, the duties and powers that are now provided in S. 495 for that office. And I would add still one more important function, that of the oversight of the execution of the laws legislated by Congress. For one of the problems that is not adequately addressed by Congress now is that once legislation has been enacted, it tends to become a license for executive and judicial action which frequently does not conform either to the language or the spirit of the laws as enacted. Some mechanism should be created to keep Congress informed, through its appropriate committees, perhaps, of what both the executive and the judicial branches of the government are doing when they allegedly enforce its laws. This function could be performed by the Office of Congressional Legal Counsel. Congress would then be in a position to redesign or restructure the governing legislation if its enforcement does not truly conform to the legislative purpose and intent at the time of enactment.

I trust that I have been helpful and not obstructive in the proposals I have made above. If there are any other particular questions that you should like me to consider, I should be happy to try to do so. But, I repeat, I do not think I can deal with your entire catalogue except cursorily, at least in the time available.

With all good wishes, as always,

Sincerely yours,

Philip B. Kurland

Senator Abe Ribicoff
Senator Charles H. Percy
Committee on Government Operations
United States Senate
Washington, D.C. 20510

PBK/s
encl.

ANNUAL CHIEF JUSTICE EARL WARREN
CONFERENCE ON ADVOCACY IN THE U.S.A./1975

Prof. Raoul Berger, Prof. Philip B. Kurland, Theodore I. Koskoff, Esq., Prof. Louis Henkin and Herbert H. Bennett, Esq.

HERBERT H. BENNETT
President
Roscoe Pound-American Trial Lawyers Foundation

THEODORE I. KOSKOFF
Chairman
Annual Chief Justice Earl Warren Conference on Advocacy

Background Papers

PROFESSOR RAOUL BERGER
Charles Warren Senior Fellow in American Legal History
Harvard Law School
Subject: PRESIDENTIAL WAR POWERS

PROFESSOR LOUIS HENKIN
Hamilton Fish Professor of International Law and Diplomacy and Professor of Constitutional Law, Columbia University School of Law
Subject: PRESIDENTIAL POWER IN FOREIGN AFFAIRS

PROFESSOR PHILIP B. KURLAND
William R. Kenan, Jr. Professor in the College and Professor of Law,
University of Chicago Law School
Subject: TOWARD A RESPONSIBLE AMERICAN PRESIDENCY

Moderators

PROFESSOR HENRY F. GRAFF

Professor of History, Columbia University; specializes in U.S. history and, within this, the history of the foreign relations of the United States and the history of the U.S. Presidency; has published extensively and is presently working on a book on the Presidency of the United States

PROFESSOR HARVEY C. MANSFIELD, SR.

Professor Emeritus of Government, Columbia University; among his numerous publications, "Arms and the State"; editor of OPA series, Historical Reports on War Administration; formerly managing editor of American Political Science Review; author of chapters, books and articles in professional journals

PROFESSOR ADAM YARMOLINSKY

Ralph Waldo Emerson Professor of the University, University of Massachusetts; served as The Special Assistant to the Secretary of Defense during the Kennedy Administration; Principal Deputy Assistant Secretary of Defense for International Security Affairs (ISA) and Deputy Director of the Anti-Poverty Task Force during the Johnson Administration

Rapporteurs

LAWRENCE M. BASKIR

General Counsel and Staff Director, President Ford's Clemency Board; Adjunct Professor of Law, Georgetown University and Catholic University; formerly Chief Counsel and Staff Director, Constitutional Rights Subcommittee, U.S. Senate

PROFESSOR HAROLD W. CHASE

Professor, Dept. of Political Science, University of Minnesota; lecturer and author of numerous articles; co-author of book, "Constitutional Interpretation: Casebook in Constitutional Law," and "Corwin's Constitution and What It Means Today," among others

W. TAYLOR REVELEY, III

Associate, Hunton, Williams, Gay & Gibson, Richmond, Va.; former International Affairs Fellow of the Council on Foreign Relations and Fellow of the Woodrow Wilson International Center for Scholars

Conferees

(Note: Titles and identifications of participants are as of the Conference date – June 20, 1975.)

LAWRENCE M. BASKIR
Washington, D.C.

General Counsel and Staff Director, President Ford's Clemency Board; Adjunct Professor of Law, Georgetown University and Catholic University; formerly Chief Counsel and Staff Director, Constitutional Rights Subcommittee, U.S. Senate

THOMAS E. CARGILL, JR.
Boston, Massachusetts

Secretary, Roscoe Pound-American Trial Lawyers Foundation; Trial Attorney

PROFESSOR GERHARD CASPER
Chicago, Illinois

Professor of Law and Political Science, University of Chicago Law School; among his writings: "On Emergency Powers of the President: Every Inch a King?", *Occasional Papers of the University of Chicago Law School;* author of book, "Realism and Political Theory in American Legal Thought" (in German)

PROFESSOR HAROLD W. CHASE
Minneapolis, Minnesota

Professor, Dept. of Political Science, University of Minnesota; lecturer and author of numerous articles; co-author of book, "Constitutional Interpretation: Casebook in Constitutional Law," and "Corwin's Constitution and What It Means Today," among others

BENJAMIN V. COHEN
Washington, D.C.

International statesman; formerly Assistant and Legal Adviser to President Franklin D. Roosevelt; legal adviser and member of international conferences following World War II, including Paris Peace Conference in 1946; author of "The United Nations Constitutional Development, Growth and Possibilities"

PROFESSOR ELMER E. CORNWELL, JR.
Providence, Rhode Island

Professor of Political Science, Brown University; teaches a course on the American Presidency; co-author of "The American Democracy," among other books

PROFESSOR THOMAS E. CRONIN
Santa Barbara, California

Visiting Professor, Dept. of Political Science, University of California (at Santa Barbara); former White House Fellow, 1966-67; author or co-author of several books including "The State of the Presidency" (1975), "The Presidency Reappraised" (1974), and "Government By The People" (1975)

PROFESSOR ANTHONY A. D'AMATO
Chicago, Illinois

Constitutional Law Professor, Northwestern University School of Law; writings include articles, monographs and chapters on international law; co-authored book, "The Judiciary and Vietnam"

GRANT DILLMAN
Washington, D.C.

Vice President and Washington Manager, United Press International; reportorial experience includes coverage of Congress and all national presidential conventions since 1948 for UPI

PROFESSOR THOMAS I. EMERSON
New Haven, Connecticut

Lines Professor of Law, Yale Law School; a constitutional theoretician of national stature, Professor Emerson's scholarly works include "The System of Freedom of Expression" and "Toward a General Theory of the First Amendment"

LOUIS FISHER
Washington, D.C.

Specialist, American National Government, Government and General Research Division, Congressional Research Service, The Library of Congress; among his publications are the books, "President and Congress: Power and Policy" and "Presidential Spending Power"

SCOTT GINSBURG
Washington, D.C.

Legislative Assistant to United States Senator Dick Clark

PROFESSOR HENRY F. GRAFF
New York, New York

Professor of History, Columbia University; specializes in U.S. history and, within this, the history of the foreign relations of the United States and the history of the U.S. Presidency; has published extensively and is presently working on a book on the Presidency of the United States

PROFESSOR J. DAVID GREENSTONE
Chicago, Illinois

> Chairman, Dept. of Political Science, University of Chicago; writings on urban affairs include his book, "Labor in American Politics" and "Race and Authority in Urban Politics" (with Paul Peterson)

MALCOLM D. HAWK
Houston, Texas

> Counsel, Exxon Company, U.S.A.; formerly Deputy Assistant Attorney General for Legislative Affairs, U.S. Department of Justice; formerly Minority Counsel, Committee on the Judiciary, U.S. Senate

PROFESSOR SAMUEL B. HOROVITZ
Boston, Massachusetts

> Professor, Suffolk University Law School; formerly Commissioner, National Commission on State Workmen's Compensation Laws

RALPH K. HUITT
Washington, D.C.

> Executive Director, National Association of State Universities and Land-Grant Colleges; director of study of Congress sponsored by the American Political Science Association; formerly Assistant Secretary of Health, Education, and Welfare for Legislation

SCOTT F. HUTCHINSON
Portland, Maine

> President, Canal National Bank, Maine

HERBERT E. KAPLOW
Washington, D.C.

> Reporter, ABC News, American Broadcasting Company; formerly reporter for NBC News, National Broadcasting Company; academic background includes degree in history

ROBERT K. KELLEY
Washington, D.C.

> Staff Lawyer, Select Committee to Study Governmental Operations with Respect to Intelligence Activities, United States Senate

PROFESSOR LOUIS W. KOENIG
New York, New York

> Professor of Government, New York University; formerly with the U.S. Dept. of State and also a member of the Foreign Affairs Task Force of the First Hoover Commission; among his publications is "The Chief Executive," now in its third edition

HONORABLE JAMES R. MANN
Washington, D.C.

> Member of Congress, U.S. House of Representatives; member of the U.S. House Judiciary Committee and its Subcommittees on Crime and Criminal Justice

PROFESSOR HARVEY C. MANSFIELD, SR.
New York, New York

> Professor Emeritus of Government, Columbia University; among his numerous publications, "Arms and the State"; editor of OPA series, Historical Reports on War Administration; formerly managing editor of American Political Science Review; author of chapters, books and articles in professional journals

IRENE R. MARGOLIS
Washington, D.C.

> Staff Director, Subcommittee on Separation of Powers of the U.S. Senate Committee on the Judiciary

PROFESSOR DAVID R. MAYHEW
New Haven, Connecticut

> Associate Professor, Dept. of Political Science, Yale University; his principal publications are "Party Loyalty among Congressmen" and "Congress: The Electoral Connection"

PROFESSOR HENRY P. MONAGHAN
Boston, Massachusetts

> Professor of Law, Boston University School of Law

JAMES M. NAUGHTON*
Washington, D.C.

White House Correspondent, *The New York Times,* Washington Bureau; has reported on the rise and fall of Vice President Spiro T. Agnew, the Senate Watergate hearings and the impeachment proceedings against President Nixon before the U.S. House Judiciary Committee

RODERICK NORDELL
Boston, Massachusetts

Assistant Chief Editorial Writer, *The Christian Science Monitor;* formerly reporter, book editor, and arts editor for the *Monitor*

HONORABLE CHARLES A. POMEROY
Portland, Maine

Associate Justice, Supreme Judicial Court, State of Maine

W. TAYLOR REVELEY, III
Richmond, Virginia

Associate, Hunton, Williams, Gay & Gibson; former International Affairs Fellow of the Council on Foreign Relations and Fellow of the Woodrow Wilson International Center for Scholars

PROFESSOR JOHN P. ROCHE
Medford, Massachusetts

Henry R. Luce Professor of Civilization and Foreign Affairs, The Fletcher School of Law and Diplomacy, Tufts University; syndicated political columnist; has written extensively on government; publications include "Sentenced to Life: Essays on Law, Politics and Education"; Special Consultant to the U.S. President, 1966-68

QUINCY RODGERS
Washington, D.C.

Minority Counsel, Subcommittee on Separation of Powers, U.S. Senate Committee on the Judiciary, and Legislative Counsel to Senator Charles McC. Mathias on U.S. Senate Judiciary Committee matters, including constitutional issues, criminal laws and administrative practice

ANTONIN SCALIA
Washington, D.C.

Assistant Attorney General, Office of Legal Counsel, U.S. Department of Justice

JERROLD L. SCHECTER
Washington, D.C.

Diplomatic Editor, *TIME* Magazine

PROF. ARTHUR M. SCHLESINGER, JR.
New York, New York

Historian; Albert Schweitzer Professor of the Humanities, The City University of New York; author of numerous books relating to the American government among which are "A Thousand Days: John F. Kennedy in the White House" and "The Imperial Presidency"

PROFESSOR HERMAN SCHWARTZ
Buffalo, New York

Professor of Law, State University of New York at Buffalo, School of Law; specialist in criminal law; consultant and adviser to numerous state and federal commissions; author and lecturer on various phases of criminal law including extensive work in the area of prisoners' rights

---

*Because James Naughton is currently responsible for attempting to provide balanced reportage on the Presidency for *The New York Times,* he considered it inappropriate to vote on the recommendations. However, Mr. Naughton did participate in the discussions.

KENNETH E. THOMPSON
Boston, Massachusetts
Associate Editor, *Boston Herald American,*
and is also chief editorial writer and editorial
page editor

SANFORD J. UNGAR
Washington, D.C.
Washington Editor, *The Atlantic Monthly;*
formerly on the national staff of *The
Washington Post;* author of "The Papers &
The Papers: An Account of the Legal and
Political Battle over the Pentagon Papers,"
and of the forthcoming book, "FBI"

HONORABLE SIDNEY W. WERNICK
Portland, Maine
Associate Justice, Supreme Judicial Court,
State of Maine

PROFESSOR GARRY WILLS
Baltimore, Maryland
Adjunct Professor of Humanities, Johns
Hopkins University; syndicated columnist

WILLIAM MARSHALL WRIGHT
Washington, D.C.
Vice President for Government Affairs,
Eaton Corporation; formerly Assistant
Secretary of State for Congressional
Relations; formerly a senior staff member of
the National Security Council during the
Nixon and Johnson Administrations
(Director for Long-Range Planning, Officer
in Charge of African Affairs, Officer in
Charge of International Organization
Affairs); among publications, "Responsible
Restraint: An American Foreign Policy
Imperative"

PROFESSOR ADAM YARMOLINSKY
Boston, Massachusetts
Ralph Waldo Emerson Professor of the
University, University of Massachusetts;
served as The Special Assistant to the
Secretary of Defense during the Kennedy
Administration; Principal Deputy Assistant
Secretary of Defense for International
Security Affairs (ISA) and Deputy Director
of the Anti-Poverty Task Force during the
Johnson Administration

Conference Observer

SISTER ROSITA UHEN
Racine, Wisconsin
Project Consultant
WINGSPREAD CENTER
The Johnson Foundation

ESTABLISHMENT OF
THE ANNUAL CHIEF JUSTICE EARL WARREN CONFERENCE
ON ADVOCACY IN THE UNITED STATES

EARL WARREN
(March 19, 1891 — July 9, 1974)

A LEGACY.   Trustees of the Roscoe Pound-American Trial Lawyers Found
again this year were pleased to conduct the Earl Warren Conference in homage to the late
Justice of the United States.

On September 28, 1968, Earl Warren, then Chief Justice of the United States, laie
cornerstone of the Roscoe Pound-American Trial Lawyers Law and Research Cent
Cambridge, Massachusetts. At that time the Foundation announced that an Annual Chief Jι
Earl Warren Conference on Advocacy would be one of its principal activities.

For the past four years the Foundation has presented this Conference. The general purpι
each Conference is to evaluate social trends and, having done so, to make recommendatio
change in the hope that this contribution brings about positive action.

The Foundation invites leaders prominent in thought and action in the law, as w
distinguished members of other disciplines who are concerned with preserving the demo
principles of America. The findings and conclusions of each Conference are published and w
disseminated.

LIFETIME FELLOWS OF THE FOUNDATION

The Lifetime Fellows of the Roscoe Pound-American Trial Lawyers Foundation are recognized for their support of research endeavors in the intensive pursuit of truth and justice for all, now, and in time to come.

James S. Abatiell
Rutland, Vt.
Abedon, Michaelson & Stanzler
Providence, R.I.
James H. Ackerman
Long Beach, Calif.
Samuel H. Adams
W. Palm Beach, Fla.
Hon. Anthony A. Alaimo
Brunswick, Ga.
Frederick W. Allen
Peoria, Ill.
George E. Allen, Jr.
Richmond, Va.
Morgan P. Ames
Stamford, Conn.
G. Ross Anderson, Jr.
Anderson, S.C.
Thomas T. Anderson
Indio, Calif.
W.H. Anderson Company
Cincinnati, Ohio
Ashcraft & Gerel
D.C.
Fielding Atchley
Chattanooga, Tenn.
Ausley, Ausley, McMullen,
O'Bryan, Michaels & McGehee
Tallahassee, Fla.
Robert E. Austin, Jr.
Leesburg, Fla.
I. Duke Avnet
Baltimore, Md.
William I. Aynes
Atlanta, Ga.
Hon. Howard Babcock
Las Vegas, Nev.
William B. Baggett
Lake Charles, La.
Nathan Baker
Hoboken, N.J.
Russell M. Baker
Dallas, Tex.
Leonard A. Baldwin
Savannah, Ga.
Hon. Joseph G. Barbieri
Elizabeth, N.J.
A. William Barlow
Honolulu, Hawaii
Hon. Frank R. Bayger
Buffalo, N.Y.

Walter C. Beall
Cincinnati, Ohio
Walter H. Beckham, Jr.
Coral Gables, Fla.
Chester Bedell
Jacksonville, Fla.
Nathan Bedell
Jacksonville, Fla.
Robert G. Beloud
Upland, Calif.
Matthew Bender & Company
New York, N.Y.
Herbert H. Bennett
Portland, Me.
Ralph R. Benson
Hollywood, Calif.
I. Joseph Berger
Cleveland, Ohio
Sydney L. Berger
Evansville, Ind.
John Berry and Andrew J. O'Connor
Ottawa, Ill.
Charles F. Blanchard
Raleigh, N.C.
Melvin Block
Brooklyn, N.Y.
Milton M. Blumenthal
Chicago, Ill.
James F. Boccardo
San Jose, Calif.
Ernst W. Bogusch
Watertown, Mass.
George A. Boyle
Bakersfield, Calif.
Bradley & Drendel
Reno, Nev.
Ellis B. Brannon
Cleveland, Ohio
Erle Bridgewater, Jr.
Athens, Ohio
Hon. Paul W. Brightmire
Tulsa, Okla.
Louis T. Brindisi
Utica, N.Y.
Walter W. Brooks
Columbia, S.C.
Horace G. Brown
Camden, N.J.
James L. Brown
Farmington, N. Mex.
M.J. Bruckner
Lincoln, Nebr.

Robert Louis Bucciere
Cincinnati, Ohio
Samuel Bucklew
Tampa, Fla.
John A. Burgess
Montpelier, Vt.
James G. Butler
Los Angeles, Calif.
Charles M. Cable
Kennett, Mo.
Callaghan & Company
Chicago, Ill.
Evan H. Callanan
Westland, Mich.
Lawrence P. Canyock
Sterling Heights, Mich.
Richard J. Cardali
New York, N.Y.
Thomas E. Cargill, Jr.
Boston, Mass.
Jessie B. Carnevale
Las Vegas, Nev.
Rex Carr
East St. Louis, Ill.
Robert E. Cartwright
San Francisco, Calif.
Thomas V. Cassidy
Peoria, Ill.
Clinton W. Chapman
D.C.
Samuel Charfoos
Southfield, Mich.
Stanley M. Chesley
Cincinnati, Ohio
Neil H. Chonin
Miami, Fla.
John L. Cifelli
Chicago, Ill.
Edward H. Cloutier
Livermore Falls, Me.
Authur Cobb
Baton Rouge, La.
Hyman J. Cohen
D.C.
Joseph Cohen
Kansas City, Kans.
Seymour L. Colin
New York, N.Y.
Bill Colson
Miami, Fla.

Arthur W. Combs and Thomas J. Mitchell
  Houston, Tex.
Al J. Cone
  W. Palm Beach, Fla.
Conviser Construction Company, Inc.
  Brookline, Mass.
Bobby Lee Cook
  Summerville, Ga.
Robert Cooney and Irving Stenn, Jr.
  Chicago, Ill.
James E. Coonley, II
  Hampton, Ia.
Philip H. Corboy
  Chicago, Ill.
John F. Corcoran
  Tucson, Ariz.
Joseph W. Cotchett
  San Mateo, Calif.
Jack Crenshaw
  Montgomery, Ala.
Norman E. Crouch
  Tampa, Fla.
Joseph C. DaPore
  Lima, Ohio
Roy Daubenspeck
  Plaistow, N.H.
Louis G. Davidson
  Chicago, Ill.
Earl H. Davis
  D.C.
George T. Davis
  San Francisco, Calif.
Peter A. Davis
  Ann Arbor, Mich.
Tom Davis
  Austin, Texas
William R. Davis
  Hartford, Conn.
William H. DeParcq
  Minneapolis, Minn.
DiCostanzo, Klonsky & Sergi
  Brooklyn, N.Y.
Robert R. Disbro
  Cleveland, Ohio
John E. Dolan, Jr.
  Patchogue, N.Y.
James A. Dooley
  Chicago, Ill.
Louis M. Drazin
  Red Bank, N.J.
Joseph C. Dwyer
  Olean, N.Y.
J. Robert Dyment
  San Diego, Calif.
Tom Eckhardt
  San Bernardino, Calif.
Jerome Edelman
  Brooklyn, N.Y.
Henry H. Edens
  Columbia, S.C.
Irving M. Einbinder
  Hagerstown, Md.
Gary Eisenberg
  Southfield, Mich.
Arnold B. Elkind
  New York, N.Y.
Seymour L. Ellison
  San Francisco, Calif.
Emroch & Cowan & Emroch
  Richmond, Va.
J. Newton Esdaile
  Boston, Mass.
Donald J. Farage
  Philadelphia, Pa.
Moody M. Farhart
  Minot, N.D.
Millard C. Farmer, Jr.
  Newnan, Ga.

Albert S. Fein
  Philadelphia, Pa.
Samuel Fein
  Springfield, Mass.
Stanley L. Feldstein
  Old San Juan, P.R.
Arnold Felton
  Boston, Mass.
Ray Ferrero, Jr.
  Fort Lauderdale, Fla.
Alfred A. Fiedler
  Omaha, Nebr.
Louis B. Fine
  Norfolk, Va.
Philip R. Finkelmeier
  Cincinnati, Ohio
Gene E. Fischer
  Fort Collins, Colo.
Joseph Lawrence Flaig
  Los Angeles, Calif.
Richard S. Fleisher
  Chicago, Ill.
Daniel Fogel
  Los Angeles, Calif.
John T. Fowler
  Berea, Ky.
John C. Frank
  Wichita, Kans.
Wesley A. Franklin
  Portland, Oreg.
Abraham E. Freedman
  Philadelphia, Pa.
Philip S. Frey
  Honolulu, Hawaii
Lawrence B. Friedman
  N. Miami Beach, Fla.
Marcus L. Friedman
  Toledo, Ohio
Hon. Jacob D. Fuchsberg
  New York, N.Y.
Samuel C. Gainsburgh
  New Orleans, La.
Harry A. Gair
  New York, N.Y.
Neil G. Galatz
  Las Vegas, Nev.
Edward J. Gallagher, Jr.
  Waterloo, Ia.
E.S. Gallon
  Dayton, Ohio
Harold M. Gamer
  Beverly Hills, Calif.
John Gardenal
  San Francisco, Calif.
Arthur D. Gatz, Jr.
  Pittsburgh, Pa.
Gustavo A. Gelpi
  Old San Juan, P.R.
Sidney W. Gilreath
  Knoxville, Tenn.
Frederick J. Gisevius, Jr.
  New Orleans, La.
Herman B. Glaser
  New York, N.Y.
John Phillips Godfrey
  Many, La.
John Michael Goldberg
  Chicago, Ill.
Goldman & Goldman
  St. Joseph, Mo.
Goldstein, Barceloux & Goldstein
  San Francisco, Calif.
Jacob Gordon
  D.C.
Norman N. Gottlieb
  Flint, Mich.
Richard D. Grand
  Tucson, Ariz.

Burl L. Green
  Portland, Oreg.
Hyman M. Greenstein
  Honolulu, Hawaii
Herbert E. Greenstone
  Newark, N.J.
Robert L. and Jessie J. Habush
  Milwaukee, Wis.
Herbert Hafif
  Claremont, Calif.
John H. Haley, Jr.
  St. Louis, Mo.
Hillary H. Hallett
  East Alton, Ill.
Oliver W. Hasenflue
  Cleveland, Ohio
William W. Hawkins
  Kingsport, Tenn.
Milton Heller
  D.C.
Thomas L. Hennessey
  Towson, Md.
C. Richard Henriksen
  Salt Lake City, Utah
Russ M. Herman
  New Orleans, La.
Lawrence P. Hickey
  Chicago, Ill.
Ben F. Hilbun, Jr.
  Starkville, Miss.
John L. Hill
  Houston, Tex.
Arthur C. Hodgson
  Lyons, Kans.
Roscoe B. Hogan
  Birmingham, Ala.
Frank D. Holcomb
  Marietta, Ga.
John F. Holcomb
  Hamilton, Ohio
Hooker, Keeble, Dodson & Harris
  Nashville, Tenn.
H. Solomon Horan
  Louisville, Ky.
Benjamin Horn
  Dayton, Ohio
Samuel B. Horovitz
  Boston, Mass.
Ernest Hubbell
  Kansas City, Mo.
Hullverson, Richardson & Hullverson
  St. Louis, Mo.
Herbert B. Hulse
  Goldsboro, N.C.
Scott F. Hutchinson
  Portland, Me.
Charles T. Hvass
  Minneapolis, Minn.
H. Albert Hyett
  Atlantic City, N.J.
John K. Hyun
  Honolulu, Hawaii
Frank C. Ingraham
  Nashville, Tenn.
Max R. Israelson
  Baltimore, Md.
Hesper A. Jackson, Jr.
  Brooklyn, N.Y.
Howard A. Jacobs
  New Haven, Conn.
Morris I. Jaffe
  Dallas, Tex.
Frank Joseph Janik, Jr.
  Amherst, Ohio
John H. Jennings
  Evansville, Ind.
Joseph L. Jerger
  Mansfield, Ohio

110

William E. Johnson
Frankfort, Ky.
E. Stewart Jones, Jr.
Troy, N.Y.
Tom G. Jones
Franklin, Ind.
Jones & Weldon
Norwalk, Calif.
James J. Kalled
Wolfeboro, N.H.
Kaplan, Latti and Flannery
Boston, Mass.
Daniel Karlin
Chicago, Ill.
Joseph Kelner
New York, N.Y.
Sidney H. Kelsey
Norfolk, Va.
John J. Kennelly
Chicago, Ill.
Raymond H. Kierr
New Orleans, La.
Daniel J. Kirk
Santa Maria, Calif.
Frederick S. Klein
Tucson, Ariz.
Sidney B. Klovsky
Philadelphia, Pa.
Melvin L. Kodas
Kansas City, Mo.
Elmo E. Koos, Sr.
Peoria, Ill.
Theodore I. Koskoff
Bridgeport, Conn.
Lawrence L. Kotin
Chicago, Ill.
Kramer, Dillon, DeBlasio & Meagher
New York, N.Y.
Lee S. Kreindler
New York, N.Y.
Kenneth N. Kripke
Denver, Colo.
Irving Kroll
Detroit, Mich.
Myron W. Kronisch
Newark, N.J.
David H. Kubert
Philadelphia, Pa.
Norman J. Landau
New York, N.Y.
Raphael Landau
Boston, Mass.
Fred Lane
Chicago, Ill.
Samuel Langerman
Phoenix, Ariz.
Larkin, Glassman & Prager Associates, Inc.
Boston, Mass.
Shelley J. Lashkowitz
Fargo, N.Dak.
James Lawyer
Des Moines, Ia.
Verne Lawyer
Des Moines, Ia.
Lawyers Co-Operative Publishing Company
Rochester, N.Y.
Saul M. Leach
Detroit, Mich.
D. Lee
Madisonville, Tenn.
Leibowitz and Corradino
East Orange, N.J.
Charles M. Leibson
Louisville, Ky.
Morton Leitson
Flint, Mich.
Elwood S. Levy
Philadelphia, Pa.

Levy & Smith
New Orleans, La.
John R. Lewis
Moses Lake, Wash.
Marvin E. Lewis
San Francisco, Calif.
Max M. Librach
St. Louis, Mo.
Harry H. Lipsig
New York, N.Y.
Bernard Lisman
Burlington, Vt.
Little, Brown & Company
Boston, Mass.
Theodore Lockyear, Jr.
Evansville, Ind.
McArdle, Harrington, Feeney
& McLaughlin
Pittsburgh, Pa.
Powers McGuire
Chicago, Ill.
Russell H. McGuirk
Portsmouth, N.H.
Arlo A. McKinnon
Milwaukee, Wis.
George Alexander McKray
San Francisco, Calif.
Sidney S. McMath & Henry Woods
Little Rock, Ark.
Raoul D. Magana
Los Angeles, Calif.
Philip H. Magner, Jr.
Buffalo, N.Y.
Joseph D. Maher, Jr.
Newark, N.J.
Thomas J. Malik
LaPlace, La.
George J. Malinsky
New York, N.Y.
Mandel & Wright
Perth Amboy, N.J.
Lawrence E. Manion
Clayton, Mo.
Hansford C. Mann
Terre Haute, Ind.
William Aden Mann
Chevy Chase, Md.
Benjamin Marcus
Muskegon, Mich.
Markoff, Gottlieb, Lazarus,
D'Auria & Maldonado
New York, N.Y.
Richard M. Markus
Cleveland, Ohio
Richard T. Marshall
El Paso, Tex.
Martindale-Hubbell, Inc.
Summit, N.J.
J. Conrad Maugans
Kokomo, Ind.
Joe L. Maynes
Aberdeen, S.Dak.
Leonard B. Melvin, Jr.
Laurel, Miss.
J. Jerry Merchant
Amarillo, Tex.
John P. Miller
Omaha, Nebr.
Miller, Pitt & Feldman
Tucson, Ariz.
Hugh Miracle
Seattle, Wash.
Alan S. Mirman
Norfolk, Va.
Esau J. Mishkin
Mineola, N.Y.
Daniel R. Monaco
Naples, Fla.

Paula I. Moore
New York, N.Y.
Thomas Owen Morgan
Rockville Centre, N.Y.
Alan E. Morrill
Chicago, Ill.
John C. Mullen
Chicago, Ill.
Martin J. Murphy
Colorado Springs, Colo.
William C. Murphy
Aurora, Ill.
Robert D. Myers
Phoenix, Ariz.
Harvey B. Nachman
Old San Juan, P.R.
James H. Nance
Melbourne, Fla.
Irving Nemerov
Minneapolis, Minn.
John E. Norton
Belleville, Ill.
Marshall I. Nurenberg
Cleveland, Ohio
Melvin O. Nuss
Great Bend, Kans.
Cornelius C. O'Brien, Jr.
Philadelphia, Pa.
John J. O'Connor, Jr.
Baltimore, Md.
Leo M. O'Connor
Sacramento, Calif.
James P. O'Flarity
Ft. Lauderdale, Fla.
Melvin Ogurak
Minneapolis, Minn.
Dr. Jack H. Olender
D.C.
George A. Osborne
San Francisco, Calif.
Nat P. Ozmon
Chicago, Ill.
Robert G. Page
New York, N.Y.
Roger L. Pardieck
Seymour, Ind.
Parker, Battaglia, Parker, Ross and Stolba
St. Petersburg, Fla.
Paty, Lawrence & Lawrence
Chattanooga, Tenn.
R.W. Payne, Jr.
Miami, Fla.
Richard W. Pectol
Johnson City, Tenn.
Rudolph T. Pelletier
Madawaska, Me.
George and Ruth Pellettieri
Trenton, N.J.
Stephen Andrew Perel
Houston, Tex.
Norman Perl
Minneapolis, Minn.
Peter Perlman
Lexington, Ky.
Theodore D. Peterson
Pasco, Wash.
Eugene H. Phillips
Winston-Salem, N.C.
Harry M. Philo
Detroit, Mich.
Harry M. Pippin
Williston, N.Dak.
Edward I. Pollock
Los Angeles, Calif.
Maurice Pope
St. Joseph, Mo.
Frank Pozzi
Portland, Oreg.

Paul L. Pratt
East Alton, Ill.
Stanley E. Preiser
Charleston, W.Va.
Jack D. Quarant
Elizabethtown, Ill.
James G. and Vivian Quinn
Oakland, Calif.
J. Ward Rafferty
New London, Conn.
Jacob Rassner
New York, N.Y.
Frank Reiss
New York, N.Y.
Eugene A. Rerat
Minneapolis, Minn.
Louis J. Richman, Jr.
Newport News, Va.
Leonard M. Ring
Chicago, Ill.
Leon RisCassi
Hartford, Conn.
Dean A. Robb
Traverse City, Mich.
Michael L. Robins
Los Angeles, Calif.
Solly Robins
St. Paul, Minn.
Robins & Meshbesher Singer & Spence
Minneapolis, Minn.
Edward B. Rood
Tampa, Fla.
Milton D. Rosenberg
Washington, Pa.
Arthur Roth
Miami, Fla.
Saul I. Ruman
Hammond, Ind.
John W. Russell
Carlinville, Ill.
Stanley E. Sacks
Norfolk, Va.
E.B. Sahlstrom
Eugene, Oreg.
Murray Sams, Jr.
Miami, Fla.
Daniel H. Sandberg
Sacramento, Calif.
Camille F. Sarrouf
Boston, Mass.
John Burley Scales
Boonville, Ind.
David Schack
New York, N.Y.
Charles Kane Schanker
Fairfax, Va.
Joseph Schneider
Boston, Mass.
Warren C. Schrempp
Omaha, Nebr.
Charles P. Scully
San Francisco, Calif.
Albert W. Seaman
Perth Amboy, N.J.
Harold A. Sherman
Perth Amboy, N.J.
Perry J. Shertz
Wilkes-Barre, Pa.
George E. Shibley
Long Beach, Calif.
Samuel Shore
Los Angeles, Calif.
Stan Siegel
Aberdeen, S.Dak.
Alan Sieroty
Sacramento, Calif.
Seymour A. Sikov
Pittsburgh, Pa.

Howard Silver
Southfield, Mich.
Moses I. Simon
Beverly, Mass.
Sinas, Dramis, Brake & Turner
Lansing, Mich.
Milton G. Sincoff
New York, N.Y.
Sindell, Sindell, Bourne, Stern & Spero
Cleveland, Ohio
Abner R. Sisson
Boston, Mass.
Cawood Smith
Harlan, Ky.
Charles W. Smith
Saco, Me.
J. Ron Smith
Lakeland, Fla.
Lester Berry Smith, Jr.
Peoria, Ill.
Smith and Munson
Chicago, Ill.
Smith and Ransom
Albuquerque, N.Mex.
Richard N. Solman
Caribou, Me.
Harold Soshnick
Shelbyville, Ind.
Craig Spangenberg
Cleveland, Ohio
Howard A. Specter
Pittsburgh, Pa.
Herbert M. Spector
Rock Island, Ill.
Stuart M. Speiser
New York, N.Y.
J.B. Spence
Miami, Fla.
Warren C. Stack
Charlotte, N.C.
Franklin C. Stark
Oakland, Calif.
Robert K. Steinberg
Beverly Hills, Calif.
Israel Steingold
Norfolk, Va.
Stewart & DeChant Company, L.P.A.
Cleveland, Ohio
Herbert F. Stride
Chicago, Ill.
Robert C. Strodel
Peoria, Ill.
Jerry H. Summers
Chattanooga, Tenn.
William Lawrence Summers
Cleveland, Ohio
Edward M. Swartz
Boston, Mass.
Glenn J. Tabor
Valparaiso, Ind.
Daniel B. Tallon
Glens Falls, N.Y.
Grace Wilkey Thomas
Atlanta, Ga.
John B. Tittmann
Albuquerque, N.Mex.
William Tomar
Camden, N.J.
Earl C. Townsend, Jr.
Indianapolis, Ind.
Jack A. Travis
Jackson, Miss.
Traxler, Malkoff & Boyd Company, L.P.A.
Youngstown, Ohio
Edward E. Triviz
Las Cruces, N.Mex.
Meyer M. Ueoka
Wailuku, Hawaii

Lewis V. Vafiades
Bangor, Me.
Vance, Davies & Roberts
Seattle, Wash.
David R. Vandenberg
Klamoth Falls, Oreg.
Christopher Marce Verbiest
Detroit, Mich.
Saul T. Von Zamft
Coral Gables, Fla.
A. Ward Wagner, Jr.
W. Palm Beach, Fla.
Bill Wagner
Tampa, Fla.
Wainwright & Wainwright
Brockton, Mass.
Henry C. Walker
Shreveport, La.
Bruce Walkup
San Francisco, Calif.
H. Calvin Walter
Knoxville, Tenn.
Cullen M. Ward
Atlanta, Ga.
Rupert Warren
Buffalo, New York
Ted Warshafsky
Milwaukee, Wis.
Solomon Wasserman
Minneapolis, Minn.
Herbert Watstein
Bristol, Conn.
Hon. Charles Weiner
Philadelphia, Pa.
Harry S. Wender
D.C.
Jack H. Werchick
San Francisco, Calif.
George F. West, Jr.
Natchez, Miss.
Joseph N. Wheeler
Somerville, Mass.
Paul Whitehead
Lynchburg, Va.
Louis Wiener, Jr.
Las Vegas, Nev.
Charles A. Williams
Paducah, Ky.
David E. Williams
Richland, Wash.
Williams, Trine and Greenstein
Boulder, Colo.
Edward B. Willing
Mt. Vernon, N.Y.
Robert B. Willson
Asheville, N.C.
Samuel Winetsky
Boston, Mass.
Irving M. Wiseman
Alton, Ill.
Crescy E. Woehrel
Westmont, Ill.
Leon Wolfstone
Seattle, Wash.
Harold E. Wonnell
Columbus, Ohio
Theodore Wurmser
Louisville, Ky.
Jerome L. Yesko
Hackensack, N.J.
Howard S. Young, Jr.
Indianapolis, Ind.
Arthur C. Zief
San Francisco, Calif.
Philip C. Zimmerly
Champaign, Ill.
Irving I. Zimmerman
Woonsocket, R.I.

Annual Chief Justice Earl Warren Conference Reports

A PROGRAM FOR PRISON REFORM

Final Report including the Findings and
Recommendations of the Annual Chief
Justice Earl Warren Conference of 1972
Library of Congress Catalog Card Number: 73-75717

THE FIRST AMENDMENT AND THE NEWS MEDIA

Final Report including the Findings and
Recommendations of the Annual Chief
Justice Earl Warren Conference of 1973
Library of Congress Catalog Card Number: 73-86879

PRIVACY IN A FREE SOCIETY

Final Report including the Findings and
Recommendations of the Annual Chief
Justice Earl Warren Conference of 1974
Library of Congress Catalog Card Number: 74-19797

The Roscoe Pound-American Trial Lawyers Foundation
20 Garden Street, Cambridge, Massachusetts 02138 Tel: (617) 491-6424

THE ROSCOE POUND-AMERICAN TRIAL LAWYERS FOUNDATION

TWENTY GARDEN STREET • CAMBRIDGE • MASSACHUSETTS 02138

THE POWERS
OF THE
PRESIDENCY

2554